HAMILTON

HAMILTON

The Energetic Founder

R. B. Bernstein

OXFORD
UNIVERSITY PRESS

OXFORD
UNIVERSITY PRESS

Oxford University Press is a department of the University of Oxford. It furthers the University's objective of excellence in research, scholarship, and education by publishing worldwide. Oxford is a registered trade mark of Oxford University Press in the UK and certain other countries.

Published in the United States of America by Oxford University Press
198 Madison Avenue, New York, NY 10016, United States of America.

Library of Congress Cataloging-in-Publication Data
Names: Bernstein, Richard B., 1956– author.
Title: Hamilton : the energetic founder / R. B. Bernstein.
Description: New York, NY : Oxford University Press, [2023] |
Includes bibliographical references and index.
Identifiers: LCCN 2023006281 (print) | LCCN 2023006282 (ebook) |
ISBN 9780190081980 (hardback) | ISBN 9780190082000 (epub)
Subjects: LCSH: Hamilton, Alexander, 1757–1804. | Founding Fathers of the United States—Biography. | United States—Politics and government—1783–1809.
Classification: LCC E302.6.H2 B47 2023 (print) | LCC E302.6.H2 (ebook) |
DDC 973.4092 [B]—dc23/eng/20230214
LC record available at https://lccn.loc.gov/2023006281
LC ebook record available at https://lccn.loc.gov/2023006282

Printed by Sheridan Books, Inc., United States of America

I dedicate
this pair of books
on Alexander Hamilton and Thomas Jefferson
to my friend and colleague
Joanne B. Freeman of Yale University,
who has taught us all so much
about the Founding Guys and their world.
And I dedicate this book on Hamilton to my brother,
Steven Jay Bernstein,
in gratitude for helping me overhaul my life
at a difficult and challenging time.

CONTENTS

In this depiction of the Federal Convention's signing of the Constitution on September 17, 1787, by the noted artist and illustrator Howard Chandler Christy, Alexander Hamilton talks with insistent urgency to Benjamin Franklin (both seated at center). This painting hangs in the US Capitol.
Architect of the Capitol

PREFACE

The Energetic Founder

At the center of Howard Chandler Christy's 1937 group portrait of the Federal Convention of 1787 are two key delegates. One of the youngest, sitting like a tightly coiled spring, is talking with intensity and energy to the Convention's oldest delegate, who is listening with benign mildness. All around them, other delegates are milling about—but for the passionate young delegate, only his ideas and his effort to expound them matter. The speaking delegate is Alexander Hamilton, his youth evident despite his powdered gray hair. The listening delegate is Benjamin Franklin, his face displaying a bemused smile.

This book is an introduction to Hamilton's life, words, and acts. It views Hamilton through an array of intellectual lenses that track Hamilton's interests, concerns, and priorities: the American Revolution, politics, law and constitutionalism, economics, diplomacy and war, and honor and dueling. Binding these subjects together are Hamilton's ambitions for an independent American nation and his commitment to help create and preserve it. We conclude by examining Hamilton in retrospect, considering his complex and tangled legacies as they stand today, showing continuities and discontinuities spanning the centuries between his time and ours.

Hamilton emerges as focused on two things that he found essential to nation-making. The first was legitimate or lawful power, which a government needs to get things done lawfully; he grouped those concepts under the word *authority*. The second was *energy*, the means for a government to wield authority most effectively; to Hamilton, energy embodied secrecy, effectiveness, and dispatch, or speed. Although he was one of the conflicted and controversial band of farmers, plantation owners, merchants, lawyers, soldiers, and clergymen collectively known as the founding fathers, Hamilton stood alone in his preoccupation with authority and energy. Indeed, Hamilton was the energetic founder, for he esteemed energy in a constitutional republic and he felt the need to act with energy himself. In all these things, Hamilton was a thinking politician, who worked primarily in the practical realm of politics but who also saw and acted on the larger significance and effects of what he was doing.

Lin-Manuel Miranda's acclaimed *Hamilton: An American Musical* has transformed Hamilton's reputation in American popular culture, also triggering blowback stimulated by issues of slavery and racism. This book focuses on Hamilton as a historical figure, but it also addresses the similarities and the differences between the historical figure and the musical's title character. Its goal in exploring those connections and contradictions is to help readers sort fact from fiction. Like so many of the founding fathers, who were obsessed with their reputations in the eyes of posterity, Hamilton would want no less.

ACKNOWLEDGMENTS

I am thankful to those who have helped me along the way. I absolve them from any mistakes, errors of judgment, and wackosity remaining in these pages.

Nancy E. Toff, my peerless editor at Oxford University Press, continues to muster exemplary patience, faith, encouragement, and goading in dealing with me. Many thanks also to her colleagues at Oxford, including my excellent copyeditor, Timothy DeWerff.

I am yet again indebted to the New York University Legal History Colloquium, a group founded by Professor William E. Nelson of New York University School of Law in 1981 and presided over by him ever since. Professor Joanne B. Freeman of Yale University and I have been talking and writing about the "founding guys" for longer than either of us will willingly admit; she has taught me far more about history and the founding guys, and Alexander Hamilton in particular, than I can recount. The sage counsel and collegial friendship of Professor Charles L. Zelden of Nova Southeastern University, my scholarly brother, remain indispensable to me. That is true, as well, of other faithful friends, including Professor Felice Batlan of Chicago-Kent Law School; Professor Annette Gordon-Reed of the Harvard Law School; Dr. Maeva Marcus of the Institute for Constitutional History at the New-York Historical Society and George Washington University; the late Professor Emeritus George

Athan Billias of Clark University and his wife Margaret; Carol Berkin, professor of history emerita at Baruch College, CUNY; and many others in the community of historians and other scholars who make study of the founding guys so rewarding.

My friends, the "usual suspects" in my life, have never stinted in insight, encouragement, and patience: Phillip A. Haultcoeur; Maureen K. Phillips and Joseph Newpol; the documentarians *extraordinaire* Ron Blumer and Muffie Meyer; April Holder and Michelle Waites; Kevin Griffin and Elissa Wynn; the late and lamented Edward D. Young III, his wife, Gina Tillman-Young, and their children, Christa, Adam, Noah (and his wife Allison and their children Selah and Daniel), Luke, Mary Maya, Peter, and Moses; Molly Myers and Hasan Rizvi and their sons, Zane and Jehan; and Internet friends Karen Spisak, Natalie D. Brown, Patrick Feigenbaum, Marion Pavan, Robert K. Folkner, Philip Whitford, Cynthia E. Nowak, and Kevin J. Hutchison.

Clark's Restaurant in Brooklyn Heights was a nursery for this book and a refuge for its author. To the Sgantzos family, my deepest thanks for all that you do.

Since 2011, I have been a member of the political science department of City College of New York's Colin Powell School for Civic and Global Leadership. To CCNY's president, Vincent Boudreau; to my colleagues and friends in its department of political science, chaired by Daniel J. DiSalvo and including Bruce Cronin, Karen Struening, John Krinsky, Carlo Invernizzi Accetti, Nicholas Rush Smith, Raphaelle Khan, Dirk Moses, and Mira Morgenstern; to CCNY's Honors Program in Legal Studies, led by Andrew Rich and Jennifer Light—to all of you, and to the many CCNY students whom I have taught and from whom I have learned so much (too many to list here), I record my hope that this book's dedication is an adequate installment of the gratitude I owe you. There will be many more installments to come.

Chapter 1

Life

Alexander Hamilton traced a long, intricate journey, from his birth in the mid-1750s on the Caribbean island of Nevis to his burial at New York City's Trinity Church in 1804. Controversy swirls around the exact year (sometime between 1754 and 1758) when he was born, though we know that his birthday was January 11. A scholarly consensus has fixed his birth year as 1755, based on a Dutch probate record; the latest major biographer questions that choice, however, opting for 1757, the year that Hamilton himself believed was right.

Hamilton's mother, Rachael Fawcett (Anglicized from Faucette) Lavien, was a French Huguenot Protestant who had abandoned her marriage to the Dutch merchant Johann Michael Lavien (by whom she had had a legitimate son, Peter). Rachael first had an affair with the mapmaker Johan Jacob Cronenberg on St. Croix and then formed a relationship on St. Kitts with James Hamilton. The fourth son of Alexander Hamilton, Lord of the Grange in Ayrshire, in Scotland, James had a lineage better than his prospects. Sometime in the mid-1750s, James and Rachael had two sons out of wedlock on Nevis—James Jr. and Alexander. In 1759, Johann Lavien divorced Rachael for desertion and adultery; the divorce, granted under Dutch law, blamed the marriage's failure on Rachael, barring her from marrying anyone else. In that year, Rachael, James, and their two sons returned to St. Croix; soon afterward, James left Rachael, for reasons unknown to posterity.

Rachael sought to earn a living by setting up a small general store, and for a time she succeeded, but within a year of launching her business she and her younger son fell ill with fever. Alexander survived, but Rachael died, aged thirty-nine. After her death, a Dutch probate court awarded her scanty estate to her sole legitimate child, Peter Lavien. Disinherited because of their illegitimacy, James and Alexander were sent to live with Robert Lytton, an adult cousin from their mother's family, but that arrangement ended when Lytton hanged himself.

James and Alexander were old enough to learn trades. James was apprenticed to be a carpenter (he apparently died in 1785 or 1786 in the West Indies). After a period of education at a Hebrew school on Charlestown, Alexander was apprenticed as a clerk to Nicholas Cruger, a partner with David Beekman in the mercantile firm of Beekman & Cruger, which had business connections to the colony of New York. Though barely in his teens, Hamilton soon became Cruger's agent, dealing as an equal with adult ship captains.

Hamilton's ambitions had a wider scope than an obscure isle in the Caribbean. In his earliest surviving letter, written in 1769 to his friend Edward Stevens, Hamilton confessed that "my ambition is prevalent" and that "I would risk my life though not my station" to advance himself; that phrase, a refrain rooted in honor culture, echoed throughout his life. Hamilton ended by confessing, "I wish there was a war."[1] It was a natural desire for a boy of his age and high intelligence; the folklore of the British army and navy was rich with tales of boys who had advanced their careers through heroic wartime service.

Not war but writing gave Hamilton his opportunity to leave the Caribbean for a more interesting world. In the summer of 1772, a hurricane laid waste to St. Croix; Hamilton recorded his impressions of the disaster and his reflections on its religious significance. He published his essay, written as a letter, in the *Royal Danish American Gazette,* where it won an appreciative audience. Among Hamilton's readers was Rev. Hugh Knox, a minister who led the Presbyterian congregation of Christiansted on St. Croix. Knox was so impressed by Hamilton's literary talent and eloquent piety that he took up a collection to send Hamilton to seek an education on the mainland of British North America. Landing in Boston, Hamilton traveled to Elizabethtown, New Jersey; he carried letters of introduction from Knox to two lawyers, William Livingston and Elias Boudinot, who later played important parts in the American Revolution and in the politics of the early American republic.

After polishing his Greek and Latin at an academy in Elizabethtown, Hamilton set his sights on enrolling at the College of New Jersey (now Princeton University). He proposed to the college's board of trustees that they admit him on terms allowing him to advance his standing as quickly as he could. Viewing his ambition with doubt, the trustees turned him down. Undeterred, Hamilton approached King's College in New York City (forerunner of Columbia University), winning entry as a special student. The King's College connection brought him two lifelong friends, whom he met through William Livingston—Robert Troup, his college roommate, and John Jay, ten years his senior.

In the early years of Hamilton's American life, the scholarship boy from the Caribbean made friends and professional acquaintances who would help him become part of New York City's interlocking circles of lawyers and politicians. Not only had he found a place in colonial American society, but he soon developed an American point of view, rather than a perspective attached to a particular colony such as New York. That American perspective was central to Hamilton's intellectual and political development.

Pursuing studies for two years at King's College, Hamilton joined the war of words and arguments that had begun in the 1760s, pitting New York's Patriots against the mother country's advocates. Hamilton began by taking on the Loyalist clergyman Rev. Samuel Seabury. Writing as "A. W. Farmer" (A Westchester Farmer), Seabury sought to demolish the credibility of the First Continental Congress, which had met in Philadelphia in September and October 1774. Seabury had published two pamphlets, *Free Thoughts on the Continental Congress* and *The Congress Canvassed.* Hamilton answered Seabury in his first major political publication, *A Full Vindication of the Measures of Congress* (1774). When in early 1775 Seabury replied to Hamilton in *A View of the Controversy between Great Britain and Her Colonies,* Hamilton blasted back with *The Farmer Refuted.*

Hamilton more than equaled Seabury in his argument's substance and in his rhetorical skills. He showed his mastery of Patriot constitutional and political arguments for American rights under the unwritten British constitution. Blending angry eloquence with youthful high spirits, he pressed his case without mercy. His pamphlets previewed the slashing, cogent polemical style that he developed for the rest of his life. In 1775, his pamphlets drew the attention of New York's Revolutionary politicians.

At the same time that Hamilton was demolishing Seabury, he rescued the Loyalist president of King's College, Rev. Myles Cooper, from a Patriot mob. His spoken eloquence distracted the angry crowd, allowing Cooper to slip away. Hamilton's oratory showed no backsliding in his Revolutionary zeal. Rather, he wove together enthusiasm for the American cause with dislike for mob rule and commitment to the rule of law, values central to his politics.

In August 1775, Hamilton began serving the Revolution in deeds as well as words; he helped to remove cannons from New York's Battery, in the process braving cannonades from British ships bombarding the city. When King's College closed under pressure from the Revolution, Hamilton could not complete his undergraduate degree. (In 1784, Columbia College gave him an honorary degree.)

In early 1776, New York's provincial congress created an artillery company, naming Hamilton its commander. After months of organizing and training his artillery company, which he financed with the remainder of the funds meant to pay for his college education, in September 1776 Hamilton and his unit joined the Continental Army's retreat up Manhattan Island. One witness noted that Hamilton resembled a drummer boy rather than an officer; he saw Hamilton walking alongside one of his company's cannon, patting and talking to it as if to a favorite pet. Crossing the Hudson River to northern New Jersey with the Continental Army, Hamilton and his men distinguished themselves that winter in American victories at the battles of Trenton and Princeton.

In those battles, Hamilton attracted the attention of General George Washington, the Continental Army's commander-in-chief, who in March 1777 invited him to join his staff as an aide-de-camp with the rank of lieutenant colonel. This encounter launched a political and personal partnership between Washington and Hamilton that continued until the older man's death in 1799.

Washington found in Hamilton a highly intelligent and energetic aide skilled with his pen. Working at Washington's side, Hamilton performed many tasks. He drafted Washington's orders, dispatches to Congress, and correspondence with politicians, military allies, and other generals; he wrote in French to communicate on Washington's behalf with such French officers as the Marquis de Lafayette. He also carried out missions for Washington to New York's governor, George Clinton, and to General Horatio Gates. In addition, like Washington and other officers (including Virginia infantry captain John Marshall), Hamilton endured the Continental Army's ordeal at Valley Forge, Pennsylvania, during the winter of 1777–1778.

While serving under Washington, Hamilton closely observed the conduct of American politics at national and state levels; he focused on the general government's want of power. He soon became convinced of the need for national constitutional reform, a cause that became the centerpiece of his politics. Before anyone else, Hamilton saw that, as a nation, the United States needed a government worthy of a nation; he was eager to make his case to anyone who might listen. In 1780, for example, he set forth his ideas in a long, cogent letter to James Duane, a New York delegate to the Continental Congress; his letter argued for giving the United States the government that a new, independent nation needed and deserved.

In 1780, the American Revolution reached its low point—the discovery of the treason of General Benedict Arnold, one of Washington's most trusted officers. That September, sentries stopped a man who claimed to be an American officer named John Anderson, but "Anderson" mistook the sentries for British sympathizers and aroused their suspicions. Arresting and searching him, they found that "Anderson" was a British secret agent, Major John André, who had papers proving his guilt and revealing Arnold's treachery. Arnold commanded the vital fort at West Point; the papers found on André showed that Arnold was ready to betray that fort to the British, out of thwarted ambition and greed. André's capture unraveled the plot and exposed Arnold as a traitor. Enraged, Washington ordered Arnold's arrest, but Arnold escaped to British lines. André was tried for and convicted of espionage. When Washington ordered André's execution by hanging, however, Hamilton disputed the sentence. Impressed by André's courage and gentlemanly bearing, he tried but failed to convince Washington that André deserved an honorable death by firing squad.

That same year, Hamilton met the woman who became his wife. Elizabeth Schuyler was the second of three daughters of the New York politician and general Philip Schuyler, who had been the behind-the-scenes strategist of the American victory at the 1777 Battle of Saratoga, the turning point of the War for Independence. Elizabeth met Alexander in March when she visited Washington's headquarters in Monmouth, New Jersey; they married in December at the Schuyler family mansion in Albany, New York.

By early 1781, Hamilton was finding his service as an aide-de-camp vexing. Over the four years since 1777, when he had accepted his appointment, Hamilton's desire for a field command warred with his commitment to Washington. As often as he asked Washington for such an appointment, however, Washington declined, insisting that he needed Hamilton at headquarters. This cycle of request and refusal kept increasing Hamilton's frustration.

In February 1781, a quarrel between Hamilton and Washington spurred Hamilton to resign from Washington's staff. When his temper cooled, Washington sought to persuade Hamilton not to leave his post, but Hamilton remained obdurate, telling his friend and fellow aide James McHenry, "[Washington] shall for once at least repent his ill-humour."[2] Hamilton spent months commanding another New York artillery company, while writing newspaper essays urging broad interpretation of the Articles of Confederation's provisions governing the powers of Congress. Hamilton always was critical of the Articles, the new nation's first form of government, for its failure to give the US federal government adequate powers.

That October, Hamilton went with his unit to Yorktown, Virginia, to serve in the Revolution's climactic battle. Taking advantage of the Continental Army's rules, and invoking the aid of his friend Lafayette, Hamilton finally secured the field command that he had long hoped to have. He led the American attack on British Redoubt No. 10, capturing that pivotal position; he thus helped to make possible a decisive French-American victory. Hamilton was present for the British surrender at Yorktown; John Trumbull's painting of the surrender shows him standing with other American officers, smiling contentedly. Afterward, Hamilton traveled to Albany to rejoin his wife; there, he left active military service with the rank of colonel.

In early 1782, Hamilton began intensive study of New York law; he drafted for himself an outline of New York's law of practice and procedure that young lawyers were still studying decades later. That July, he won admission to the state bar, under a rule that exempted

For their artistic brilliance and their ability to capture his friend's intelligence and character, John Trumbull's portraits of Alexander Hamilton are generally regarded as the best we have. *Detroit Publishing Company photograph collection, Library of Congress, LC-DIG-det-4a26166*

army veterans from the usual three years of legal apprenticeship. By 1784, he had established a thriving legal practice in New York City. He argued such cases as *Rutgers v. Waddington* (1784), representing Loyalists sued by New Yorkers under the state's Trespass Act or suing to recover debts that New York debtors owed to his clients. He also wrote essays under the pen name Phocion (an Athenian statesman known for his honesty even when unpopular), arguing against state statutes punishing Loyalists.

In 1782, Robert Morris, the Confederation's superintendent of finance and a sympathetic recipient of a Hamilton letter on constitutional reform, named Hamilton receiver of Continental requisitions for New York. It was a thankless post, as the state failed to meet its financial obligations to the Confederation by declining to meet the voluntary requisitions sought from the states by the Confederation, but Hamilton's service as receiver intensified his commitment to revising or replacing the Articles. So did the New York legislature's choice of Hamilton to represent the state in the Confederation Congress. There he allied himself with Virginia delegate James Madison, his ally on constitutional reform through the 1780s.

In February 1783, Hamilton learned that disgruntled Continental Army officers were planning to use the army to pressure Congress to meet their demands for their deferred pay; he suggested to Washington that the general take advantage of the officers' discontent to induce Congress to do justice to the army. Washington rejected Hamilton's suggestion as improper. In March, he thwarted the officers' planned rebellion, confronting them at the army's headquarters in Newburgh, New York. (The failed plot was known thereafter as the Newburgh Conspiracy.)

Unfazed by Washington's rejection of his suggestion, Hamilton continued his mix of politics, law practice, and civic engagement. In 1785 he helped to organize the Society for Promoting the Manumission of Slaves. This group's purpose was to persuade slaveowners to free their slaves, rather than seeking slavery's abolition by law. In 1787, as part of his work for the Manumission Society, he joined John Jay and others to found the first African free school in New York City.

In 1786, Hamilton won election to the New York state assembly, the first of only two elective offices he held. That year, New York's legislature chose him to be a New York delegate to a commercial convention scheduled to meet in Annapolis, Maryland. Only twelve delegates from five states arrived in Annapolis by September 11, the convention's scheduled first day. At first, most of his colleagues were dismayed by how few delegates were there to represent so few states. By contrast, Hamilton seized the opportunity posed by the Annapolis Convention. He urged that the delegates build on the convention's stated purpose. Working with Madison, a fellow delegate from Virginia, Hamilton drafted the convention's report to Congress and the several states. In a classic lawyer's move, he gained control of the political future by writing the document that would shape future events.

Hamilton's report explained that the Annapolis Convention's goal—reforming the Confederation's lack of power over interstate commerce—was not enough. Putting aside the Annapolis Convention's failure, he recommended calling another convention—a general convention that would meet in Philadelphia in May 1787, with the goal of rendering the structure of American government adequate to the needs of the Union. The delegates endorsed his proposal, adopted his report, sent copies to the states and to Congress, and adjourned—though delegations from four states were still on their way to Annapolis. (The other four states never sent delegates.) Hamilton's report made the general convention and its mandate the focus of national politics. Even before Congress acted, six states voted to appoint delegates to the convention that Hamilton proposed. On February 21, 1787, the Confederation Congress finally responded to Hamilton's report, endorsing the Federal Convention, though limiting that convention's mandate to revising the Articles; six other states adopted resolutions inspired by the Confederation Congress and choosing delegates on that basis. Only Rhode Island, the Confederation's smallest state, refused to act.

As New York's leading advocate of national constitutional reform, Hamilton was a natural choice to represent his state in the Federal Convention. Governor George Clinton and his allies were content, however, with New York's advantageous position as a wealthy, powerful state in a weak confederation. Seeing no reason to disturb New York's position in American politics, the state's legislature followed Clinton's lead, choosing Judge Robert Yates and Mayor John Lansing Jr. of Albany to represent New York along with Hamilton. Because they were Clintonians committed to New York's interests, Yates and Lansing regularly outvoted the nationalist Hamilton.

For several weeks, Hamilton nursed his growing frustration with his position in the Convention. On June 18, 1787, he yielded to his temptation to hold forth. Taking the floor, he gave a speech between three and six hours in length. He mocked the Articles of Confederation and the delegates' plans to fix them. Instead, he described his own plan for a truly national government that would have reduced the states to administrative districts and vested the general government with sweeping national powers. Unfortunately for Hamilton, his proposal remained only a proposal. He could only declaim and argue, for Yates and Lansing would not support his proposal on behalf of New York, nor would anybody else in the Convention, not even Madison. His speech impressed the delegates, but convinced no one.

By late June, none of New York's delegates felt comfortable in the Convention. All three New Yorkers left Philadelphia by July 10 to return home. Yates and Lansing left to report to Governor Clinton their failure to restrain the Convention; Hamilton went home to resume practicing law. In September, Hamilton returned to Philadelphia, to ensure that the proposed Constitution would bear at least one New Yorker's signature, even though he lacked authority to sign. Admitting that the proposed Constitution did not go as far as he would go in giving the United States a powerful general government, he still insisted that the Constitution offered a chance of good that he would work to secure.

Though he had found his experience at Philadelphia disappointing, Hamilton was determined to work hard for the Constitution's ratification in 1787 and 1788. A leader of the forces backing the Constitution (Federalists), he fought to elect Federalist delegates to New York's ratifying convention and to make the case for the Constitution in the national war of paper and ink. The argument over the Constitution produced broadsides plastered on walls, newspaper essays, pamphlets—and even a book.

That book was a full defense of the Federal Convention and the proposed Constitution, as well as a scorched-earth assault on the Articles of Confederation. Hamilton, John Jay (the Confederation's secretary for foreign affairs), and James Madison (a Virginia delegate to the Confederation Congress and, like Hamilton, a framer and signer of the Constitution) wrote *The Federalist* as a newspaper column appearing twice a week in New York City's newspapers. They wrote eighty-five essays under the alias Publius, a pen-name from Roman history standing for sound political building. Hamilton wrote fifty-one essays, Madison wrote twenty-six, Jay wrote five, and Hamilton and Madison collaborated on three. Though Federalists valued the essays as a debater's handbook, *The Federalist* exerted its main influence on American constitutional and political thought only after the Constitution's adoption in 1788.

New York elected sixty-five delegates to its ratifying convention —of whom forty-six opposed the Constitution and only nineteen (including Hamilton and Jay) backed it. The Constitution's supporters, however, outdid their opponents in determination, energy, and shrewdness. New York's ratifying convention convened in Poughkeepsie in June 1788. By then, eight states had ratified the Constitution and none had rejected it; two other ratifying conventions also were meeting in June, in New Hampshire and Virginia. Hamilton (having won his second elective office as a Federalist delegate from New York City) became the Federalists' floor leader in Poughkeepsie.

Political calculations drove the Federalists at Poughkeepsie to favor such delaying tactics as clause-by-clause debate of the Constitution (though Anti-Federalists also welcomed such debate to air what they saw as the Constitution's flaws). Meanwhile, Hamilton and his colleagues awaited news from Concord and Richmond, where the New Hampshire and Virginia conventions were hard at work. When news of the ninth and tenth states' ratifications confirmed the Constitution's adoption as the new form of government for the United States, the issue in Poughkeepsie was no longer whether New York would ratify the Constitution, but whether New York would stay in the Union by ratifying the Constitution or leave the Union by rejecting it.

As the delegates faced external pressure to ratify, New York City brought internal pressure to bear as well. The residents of the city, the nation's capital under the Confederation, threatened to secede from New York State and join the Union as its capital. New York City's threat increased the stakes in Poughkeepsie. While Hamilton argued for ratification on the convention floor, Jay worked behind the scenes to back the Constitution by wooing wavering Anti-Federalists. Finally, on July 26, 1788, led by the Anti-Federal floor leader, Melancton Smith, the New York delegates voted narrowly for ratification, 30–27.

In the transitional period between the end of government under the Confederation and the launch of government under the Constitution, Hamilton advised Washington, the incoming first president, how to conduct himself to preserve his and the presidency's dignity. He also worked to ensure that no one—in particular the first vice president, John Adams—could challenge Washington for preeminence. After Washington was inaugurated as president, Hamilton worked confidentially to help craft the federal statute establishing the Treasury department and its chief office, secretary of the Treasury. Once that bill became law, President Washington nominated Hamilton as secretary of the Treasury and the Senate confirmed him.

The challenges facing Secretary Hamilton were daunting. The United States had amassed staggering debts during the Revolution and under the Confederation. Could the new nation manage its burden of debt, let alone repay it? What others feared as an insurmountable obstacle, Hamilton saw as a challenge. He would not have to deal with the government's funds; rather, he would help to set public policy under the Constitution and administer his department, including writing reports on the public credit at Congress's behest. Hamilton understood that duty with a lawyer's wisdom: writing such reports would empower him, not restrict him.

Hamilton seized the chance presented by a memorial from Pennsylvania creditors to the First Federal Congress urging the federal government to pay the United States' full outstanding debt. Viewing the matter as explosively controversial, a House committee chaired by Madison referred the memorial to Hamilton, who welcomed this opportunity to shape events.

In his first report on the public credit, which he made public in January 1790, Hamilton argued that the nation should pay its full debt as a matter of national honor. Indeed, he added, the federal government also should assume the states' outstanding debts, consolidating them with the national debt. The government would then pay off the consolidated debt—but not all at once. Rather, Hamilton wrote, the consolidated debt would become a fund, a continuing obligation. The government would use part of the national revenue to retire interest and part of the principal of the debt at regular intervals. This method would put more capital into circulation; the federal government would issue certificates as currency substitutes, increasing federal money in circulation and stimulating economic growth while showing Congress's commitment to pay the consolidated national debt. Hamilton's plan drew on fiscal policies adopted by Great Britain under Sir Robert Walpole's leadership, but with modifications tailored to the American situation.

Hamilton's program provoked passionate debate. Leading opponents of his plan, led by Rep. James Madison of Virginia, denounced Hamilton's proposal because, they charged, it would benefit speculators in Confederation debt while injuring widows and war veterans on whom those speculators preyed. Madison and his allies also claimed that Hamilton's policies would undermine republican government by promoting speculation and fiscal manipulation. Other objectors sought favorable treatment for their states' debts, with little attention to the larger dimensions of the issues before the nation.

The result of this bitter controversy was a national fiscal crisis that found solution only through the Compromise of 1790. Three factors contributed to establishing that compromise—the issue of the location of the permanent national capital and the entry into the controversy by Secretary of State Thomas Jefferson and by Pennsylvania senator Robert Morris. Jefferson hoped to resolve a crisis that threatened to damage the nation's interests in the international economy; he also saw the benefits of a link between adopting Hamilton's program and fixing the location of the permanent national capital. That location could decide which interests would influence national policy. If the capital were to be located in a northern city such as New York or Philadelphia, northern commercial and industrial interests would shape national policy. By contrast, if the capital were sited in a new city in the agricultural South, agricultural interests would influence national policy. Senator Morris was sympathetic to Hamilton, but he had an agenda of his own. He wanted to move the capital to Philadelphia—but he favored making the capital's ten-year sojourn there last indefinitely or even permanently.

The event that led to the Compromise of 1790 was a meeting of Jefferson, Hamilton, and Madison. In that meeting, Hamilton agreed to an ultimate Southern location for a new Federal city, after a decade in Philadelphia; Madison agreed to cease his active opposition to Hamilton's program and released two Virginia representatives to vote for it. That the federal capital's final location would be along the Potomac River delighted Washington, who had long favored developing the Potomac region; it also pleased Jefferson and Madison, both of whom favored agrarian influence over national policymaking. That Madison agreed that the capital would move first from New York to Philadelphia and then after ten years to the banks of the Potomac pleased both Virginians and Senator Morris. All were contented—at first; the assumption was enacted into law and the crisis passed.

Jefferson began to have second thoughts about the Compromise of 1790—wondering whether that compromise was as good a deal as he had thought at first. That question acquired urgency when Hamilton revealed his second report on the public credit late in 1790. Hamilton now wanted the federal government to create a Bank of the United States—a central financial institution (resembling the Bank of England) that would maintain the national currency, shelter federal tax and tariff revenues, and assist the government in managing its finances. The Bank thus would help to strengthen the national economy, manage repayment of the debt, boost the economy's commercial and manufacturing components, and augment the federal government's economic powers. Horrified, Jefferson, Madison, and other political allies who favored agrarian economy condemned Hamilton's Bank as a sinkhole of corruption that would destroy liberty, sabotage honest republican government, and threaten the success of the Revolution. Hamilton's Bank plan helped to impel Jefferson from being an honest broker between Madison and Hamilton to joining Madison in opposition to Hamilton.

The brawl over the Bank focused controversy on constitutional interpretation as well as on public policy. The great national question was clear and threatening: did Congress have the power under the Constitution to create a national bank? Jefferson, Madison, and Attorney General Edmund Randolph, all Virginians, argued that such claims of congressional power would exceed those powers explicitly granted by the Constitution to the federal government. Even though both houses of Congress passed the Bank bill, the phalanx of Virginians opposing the measure rattled President Washington. After reading Jefferson's and Randolph's opinions contesting the Bank's constitutionality, he passed them to Hamilton, asking him to answer them if he could. Meanwhile, Madison was drafting a veto message for the president's signature.

In February 1791, writing at top speed, Hamilton prepared his "Opinion on the Constitutionality of the Bank" within a week and delivered it to Washington. In that document, Hamilton refuted Jefferson's and Randolph's arguments, justifying the Bank bill as constitutional. Where Jefferson took a restrictive view of federal constitutional power, arguing that no constitutional provision explicitly gave Congress power to create a bank, Hamilton read the Constitution broadly as giving generous grants of power to Congress—both powers explicitly granted and powers implied by explicit grants of power and explicit statements of purpose of powers. The only limit on Congress, Hamilton insisted, would be a clause explicitly denying Congress power to create a Bank—but no such clause existed, so Congress could act. Relieved by Hamilton's Opinion justifying the Bank bill's constitutionality, Washington signed the Bank bill into law. But Washington's acceptance of Hamilton's argument did not end the debate over the extent and limits of federal power under the Constitution; indeed, the dispute over explicit versus implied powers, restricted versus broad constitutional interpretation, continues to this day.

Only with Hamilton's 1791 *Report on Manufactures* did the Treasury Secretary's winning streak fail. In that report, Hamilton sought to expand federal economic policy to enable Congress to promote manufacturing enterprises. The methods that he suggested included levying tariffs protecting fledgling industries until they were securely established; awarding prizes for new developments in technology; restricting or banning export of raw materials; subsidizing key industries; building roads and canals—internal improvements—to tie the national economy together; adopting a system regulating the quality of manufactured products; and encouraging inventions. The historian Richard B. Morris, an acute student of Hamilton's thought, called Hamilton's *Report on Manufactures* "the Bible of those who have advocated government aid to encourage industry."[3] Seeing the *Report on Manufactures* as a bridge too far, however, Congress refused to act on it.

Hamilton's work as secretary of the Treasury had political as well as constitutional and economic consequences for the United States. Those agreeing with Jefferson and Madison in distrusting Hamilton's economic vision and constitutional views also rejected his ideas' political consequences. They feared the kinds of corruption that they associated with the Bank of England, with the promotion of speculation and commerce, and with the abandonment of a principally agrarian economy in favor of one combining agriculture, commerce, and manufacturing. These economic, constitutional, and political disagreements helped foster the splitting of the American people into two great partisan alliances, the Federalists and the Republicans. Federalists supported Washington's administration, Hamilton's policies, and broad constitutional interpretation; Republicans backed Jefferson, Madison, and their allies, agrarian economic policies, and restrictive constitutional interpretation.

Joining partisan divisions rooted in differing economic and constitutional visions were new splits growing out of foreign policy; these splits were fomented by the revolution convulsing France and alarming Europe. Seasoned observers like Jefferson saw France as plagued by decadence and corruption, but even Jefferson—an attentive student of French government, politics, and society—missed the signs of an upheaval that would rock the French nation to its core. When the French Revolution began in July 1789, with riots gripping Paris and capturing and demolishing the enormous French prison known as the Bastille, Americans did not know what to think.

In 1790, two events helped to spur American responses to the French Revolution. The Marquis de Lafayette sent the Bastille's key to President Washington as an expression of French gratitude for the inspiration of the American Revolution; it hangs to this day beside the front door of Washington's mansion at Mount Vernon. At the same time, the Irish politician and Member of Parliament Edmund Burke published his eloquent, alarmed counterrevolutionary pamphlet, *Reflections on the Revolution in France*. Burke's pamphlet triggered a host of replies extolling the French Revolution, chief among them Thomas Paine's pamphlet *Rights of Man*, Part One. Republicans linked the American and the French Revolutions as similar revolts on behalf of popular republican government; they believed that they should embrace the cause of revolutionary France as the cause of all humanity. By contrast, Federalists heeded Burke's arguments; they feared the French Revolution as an uncontrolled spasm of human emotion, a toxic convulsion threatening to destroy law, religion, stability, and good order.

Hamilton and Jefferson at first led Federalists and Republicans as rival factions motivated by clashing domestic visions. Now, their factions also supported (Republicans) or opposed (Federalists) the French Revolution and their contrasting constellations of political values. Pitting Hamilton and Jefferson against each other were two sets of powerful ideological forces, one domestic and one international. The domestic forces pitted Federalist friends of American economic and constitutional powers against Republican critics of those powers; the international forces pitted Republican supporters of the French Revolution against Federalist critics of that Revolution. The result was to intensify feelings of personal and political rivalry. Each leader felt responsible to his own cause and followers, viewing his rival's cause and followers as mistaken and dangerous. Each concluded that he was justified in taking whatever steps would counter his rival and his rival's faction. The members of each faction agreed.

One of the few points on which Hamilton and Jefferson agreed in 1792 was that George Washington should stand for re-election as president. As the 1792 election approached, Hamilton and Jefferson each told Washington that the nation needed him to serve a second term. Washington was reluctant to remain as president; he had even asked Madison to draft a farewell address for him. Nonetheless, he allowed his two leading advisors to override his personal desire to step down. That fall, he was re-elected, again unanimously, and Vice President Adams won re-election with a majority of electoral votes. Unfortunately for Washington, from 1793 to 1797 he had to endure four years of bitter partisan strife, far more stressful than his first term had been.

In 1793, trying one last time to force Hamilton out of Washington's administration, Jefferson urged Virginian representatives in the House, led by William Branch Giles, to charge Hamilton with corruption in running the Treasury department. Jefferson even framed a set of resolutions demanding a formal investigation of the Treasury, which he passed to Giles for submission to the House of Representatives. Realizing that Jefferson's draft resolutions were too extreme, Giles toned them down before introducing them in the House. Nonetheless, the House rejected Giles's milder version, ending the Republicans' threat to Hamilton's continued service as secretary of the Treasury.

Following the failure of the Giles Resolutions another controversy arose, rooted in foreign policy: what position should the United States take regarding revolutionary France? The French had deposed, tried, convicted, and executed King Louis XVI and his consort, Marie Antoinette, and abolished the monarchy, proclaiming a republic. Conservative European monarchies led by Great Britain responded by declaring war on France, and revolutionary France promptly declared war on them. President Washington and the cabinet agreed with Hamilton that the 1778 French-American treaty of alliance had been with the French king, not with the French nation, and that the king's execution had brought that alliance to an end; only Jefferson dissented. Washington therefore was free to declare American neutrality, and he issued a proclamation to that effect, relying on his authority as president. Writing in Philadelphia newspapers as Pacificus, Hamilton defended Washington's embrace of neutrality on constitutional, political, and diplomatic grounds; writing as Helvidius, Madison disputed Hamilton's position, insisting that the president could not proclaim neutrality based on his constitutional powers alone, and that Washington's neutrality proclamation also was politically and diplomatically inadvisable.

Meanwhile, the new French minister to the United States, Edmond Charles Genet, was campaigning to win American popular support for the French cause despite Washington's proclamation of neutrality; Genet even tried, as he put it, to go over the president's head to the American people. Once Genet said so, a grim President Washington, backed by his cabinet, concluded that Genet had gone too far; they asked France to recall him. Recognizing that his American efforts were doomed to fail and that his countrymen might take severe reprisals against him should he return to France, he resigned and settled in New York. Frustrated by this latest political defeat, Jefferson handed in his resignation as secretary of state. Though Washington persuaded him to delay his departure from the government more than once, Jefferson finally stepped down on January 5, 1794, returning to private life. His exit, which ended the balance in the cabinet between Jefferson and Hamilton, may have pushed Washington to align himself with Hamilton and the Federalists.

Despite Jefferson's resignation, Hamilton doubted that Jefferson would be gone from politics for good. Just as important, he and the Washington administration faced another crisis. Farmers in western Pennsylvania resented the federal tax on whiskey, which cut into the funds that they could raise for themselves by growing wheat and rye and distilling them into whiskey. They therefore opposed the federal whiskey tax. Hamilton's response was grim. Seeing their resistance as the first sign of a movement that must be destroyed lest it destroy the federal government, he persuaded Washington to muster a force of 15,000 men and to march at their head into Pennsylvania to quell the "Whiskey Rebellion." At the first sign of federal force marching to counter their resistance, the rebellious farmers dispersed; with the threat to national authority at an end, Washington returned to the nation's capital, leaving Hamilton in charge of the militia.

A few months after the quelling of the Whiskey Rebellion, explaining to Washington that he needed to shift his attention from the nation's finances to his own, "which want my attention not a little," Hamilton resigned as secretary of the Treasury on January 31, 1795; he pledged to continue to be of service to Washington when needed. Hamilton resumed practicing law in New York City. He remained an unofficial advisor to Washington, including helping to draft the president's Farewell Address in 1796. That powerful document blended disinterested statements of political principle with occasionally bitter reflections by Washington on the pointed criticisms that Republicans had made of him. Meanwhile, the 1796 election, the first contested presidential election in American history, elevated John Adams to the presidency. Finishing behind Adams by only three electoral votes, the Republican presidential candidate, Thomas Jefferson, became vice president. Jefferson wrote that he was delighted with the "honorable and easy" office of vice president, calling the presidency a "splendid misery."

In late 1796, Republicans in Congress again accused Hamilton of corruption; though a former Treasury Secretary, he was still vulnerable to political attack. In 1791 and 1792, they charged, he had engaged in speculation, drawing on his inside knowledge of the nation's finances. Though Hamilton rejected this accusation, it was how he refuted it that caused him public embarrassment and private grief. In 1797, in his pamphlet defending himself, Hamilton explained that, instead of speculating on inside information, he was paying blackmail to James Reynolds to buy his silence about

Hamilton's adulterous affair with Reynolds's wife, Maria Reynolds. Though it refuted Republican charges of speculation, Hamilton's revelation humiliated him, wounded his wife, and injured his political reputation.

President Adams kept Washington's cabinet as his own—a disastrous decision. Later, Adams admitted to Benjamin Rush that he did not know the members of Washington's cabinet well enough to judge whether he should have kept them in office; he did so because he had not wanted to seem to question Washington's judgment in appointing them. The cabinet had no loyalty to Adams, however; they were loyal to Hamilton (whom they saw as their political leader) or to Washington. They often went behind Adams's back to Hamilton for advice. Hamilton thought as little of Adams as Adams thought of him. The government had to be led, Hamilton thought, and if Adams would not lead it, Hamilton would lead it for him.

One factor prompting Hamilton to manipulate Adams's advisors was the deterioration of American relations with France. Insults to the United States by the French regime infuriated the American people; President Adams's angry response briefly made him popular. Adams joined with Federalists in Congress to prepare the United States for possible war with France. At sea, an undeclared "quasi-war" raged between American and French naval vessels. On land, the government mustered an American army, which Adams asked ex-president Washington to command. When Washington told Adams that he wanted Hamilton as his second-in-command (as inspector general), the president at first refused, irritating the ex-president, who insisted on having Hamilton in his chain of command.

Further, to bolster the government for national security reasons, Congress enacted a set of highly controversial measures, the Alien and Sedition Acts, which tightened naturalization requirements for those seeking to become naturalized citizens and which criminalized speech or published words criticizing the federal government, the president, or other federal officials. The outnumbered Republicans, including Vice President Jefferson, viewed these measures with alarm as symbolizing what Jefferson called "the reign of witches." Republicans thought that Hamilton was planning to quash them and to tyrannize over the nation, a view that troubled President Adams as well. For his part, Hamilton feared that Republicans might emulate French radicals, threatening to overthrow the American government, religion, and good order. Each side took an extreme, alarmist view of the other side's purposes and motives.

Political turbulence and the threat of worse rocked the nation. Americans on all sides worried that the conflict might grow sharp enough to shatter the constitutional system. Would the French crisis, the 1800 election, or both, fatally wound American constitutional government?

On December 14, 1799, in the midst of this storm of controversy, sixty-seven-year-old George Washington died suddenly of respiratory issues; his unexpected passing upended the American political world. When Hamilton learned of Washington's passing, he became distraught, writing to Tobias Lear, Washington's private secretary, "The very painful event . . . [news of Washington's death] . . . had, previously to the receipt of it, filled my heart with bitterness. Perhaps no man in this community has equal cause with myself to deplore the loss. I have been much indebted to the kindness of the General, and he was an Aegis very essential to me."[4] Though some have read Hamilton's letter as viewing Washington's passing selfishly, the context does not support that view. It does suggest, however, that Hamilton was so moved by Washington's death, which ended a close personal and political partnership spanning nearly twenty-five years, that he did not heed his own choice of words, a tendency that affected him throughout 1800.

Washington's death convinced Adams that he no longer had to keep Washington's cabinet as his own, especially as Adams now realized that Hamilton had been running his government behind his back. The two politicians had long despised each other; Adams had barely tolerated Hamilton's appointment as inspector general of the army. Now he refused to allow Hamilton to succeed Washington as the army's commander. And more developments injurious to Hamilton were on the way.

In the spring of 1800, Adams told his cabinet that, rather than keeping the United States on a war footing against France, he would negotiate a new treaty with France and disband the army, which had been raised to meet a French threat that did not exist. He also forced Secretary of War James McHenry to resign, fired Secretary of State Timothy Pickering, and confined Treasury Secretary Oliver Wolcott to the duties of his office, until Wolcott resigned by year's end. Adams replaced them with men loyal to him. Hamilton and Adams quarreled loudly and bitterly about Adams's plans to end the French crisis, each convinced that the other was mad.

Infuriated, Hamilton wrote *A Letter Concerning the Character and Conduct of the Hon. John Adams, Esq. President of the United States* (1800). He hoped to distribute his vehement pamphlet only to leading Federalists, to persuade them to abandon Adams in the Electoral College for Charles Cotesworth Pinckney, the Federalist candidate for vice president, whom Hamilton saw as more willing to listen to him. His diatribe leaked beyond his intended audience, however, generating blowback damaging to both Hamilton and Adams.

The uproar persuaded Hamilton's Federalist friends that his pamphlet and his decision to go ahead with it proved that he lacked the judgment that a political leader should have. In another impulsive move, Hamilton tried to persuade Governor John Jay to secure some of New York's Electoral College votes for the Federalists, but Jay wrote on Hamilton's letter, "Proposing a measure for party purposes which it would not become me to adopt," and he filed it away without answering it.[5] Again, in his injudicious letter, Hamilton had showed questionable judgment under political pressure.

The 1800 election's results left Hamilton aghast. Republicans captured both houses of Congress. Worse still, Hamilton's national political rival, Thomas Jefferson, tied with his New York political rival, Aaron Burr, for the presidency; under the Constitution, the lame-duck House of Representatives, dominated by Federalists, would choose the winner. Pinckney, Hamilton's choice to replace Adams, had finished fourth, out of the running. Hamilton therefore begged Federalists to back Jefferson to break the electoral deadlock with Burr. Unlike Burr, he argued, Jefferson had principles, even if Federalists disliked them; by contrast, he insisted, Burr was governed only by his own ambition. Federalists, who for a time had been tempted to back Burr over Jefferson (whom they saw as a partisan fanatic), refused to listen to Hamilton.

Hamilton thus had no influence over the wrangles in the House to resolve the electoral tie between Jefferson and Burr. Instead, in a series of intricate partisan maneuvers, some Federalists cast blank ballots, and the House voted to give Jefferson the victory on its thirty-sixth ballot. Coming in second, Burr became vice president—but Jefferson and his supporters now so distrusted Burr, based on his maneuverings with Republicans and Federalists, that they denied him any influence in the new administration.

Because the results of the 1800 election eclipsed him as a Federalist political leader, Hamilton busied himself with his law practice; with writing editorials (behind the scenes) for the *New-York Evening Post* (including one in 1803 applauding the Louisiana Purchase while scolding Jefferson for abandoning his restrictive constitutional principles in making the deal); with caring for his wife and children; and with building the Grange, the only house he ever owned, in Upper Manhattan. At one point, he wrote wryly, "A garden, you know, is a very usual refuge of a disappointed politician."[6]

In 1801, a collision between politics and family, with roots in the 1800 election, devastated Hamilton. His eldest son, Philip, had fallen into a bitter personal and political controversy with an adherent of Aaron Burr, George Eacker. Their honor dispute led to a duel in which Eacker mortally wounded Philip. Though Hamilton had tried to advise Philip on a general approach to honor disputes, he did not manage to guide his son safely through the conflict with Eacker. Philip's death cast a bleak shadow over Hamilton's last years; portraits of him painted by Ezra Ames show him beset by melancholy and middle age. But Hamilton was not done with dueling and politics, nor were they done with him.

During his time on Washington's staff and later as a national politician, Hamilton always had been sensitive to real or imagined slurs against his honor. Sometimes he took offense at another gentleman's words; sometimes his words proved offensive to another gentleman who sought to take issue with him. In most cases, these honor disputes found negotiated resolutions. In June 1804, however, Hamilton faced an honor dispute for which there was no peaceful resolution.

That spring, New Yorkers faced that year's election for governor of the state. Burr put himself forward as the gubernatorial candidate of the state's faction of Burrite Republicans; to Hamilton's horror, the state's Federalists then chose Burr as their candidate. Hamilton worked against Burr's candidacy. Clintonian Republicans stood behind their nominee, Morgan Lewis, who easily defeated Burr. Angered by his defeat, Burr determined that he would pick an honor dispute in his own defense against the first man of distinction on the other side to declare himself. Burr got his chance when he read a letter in the *Albany Argus* newspaper in which a Federalist, Dr. Charles Cooper, wrote to Hamilton's father-in-law, General Philip Schuyler, that Hamilton held a "despicable opinion" of Burr. Burr sent Hamilton a demand that he either explain or apologize for that opinion. After two weeks of acrimonious letters that did not resolve the dispute between them, Burr demanded that Hamilton apologize for every negative opinion of Burr that he had expressed since 1789, and that he never voice another. Hamilton retorted that no man with honor could give such an undertaking. Burr therefore challenged Hamilton to a duel, and Hamilton accepted that challenge. Both men were acting under the pressures of honor culture interacting with politics in the theater of public opinion. This dispute was the apex of a series of clashes between them going back to 1789.

In a letter written to his wife Elizabeth on July 10, 1804, the night before the duel, Hamilton declared that he knew that Elizabeth would accept his willingness to risk his life to preserve his honor—an echo of his 1769 letter to Edward Stevens. He also revealed his decision to fire into the air and not at Burr, a choice that he otherwise kept to himself.

On the morning of July 11, Burr and Hamilton met on the dueling ground at Weehawken, New Jersey, with their seconds, William P. Van Ness and Nathaniel Pendleton, and a doctor, David Hosack. In the duel, Hamilton fired into the air, but Burr mortally wounded Hamilton. Pendleton and Dr. Hosack rowed Hamilton back across the Hudson River and carried him to a friend's house on Jane Street in Manhattan's Greenwich Village. After more than a day of terrible suffering, Hamilton died on the afternoon of July 12, 1804.

Chapter 2

Revolution and Politics

Revolution and politics were concepts inextricably linked in Alexander Hamilton's thought. For Hamilton, revolution meant, first and foremost, the American Revolution, which in his mind and heart stood for American independence, as goal and then as result. As Hamilton saw it, victory in the American Revolution would bring about both American independence and a uniquely American form of politics for an independent American nation. Indeed, Hamilton understood the creation of that independent American nation to be, at its core, a matter of politics—of political thought, argument, and action.

Hamilton had a complicated engagement with the idea of revolution, in theory and in practice. Shaping that engagement were his lifetime's two revolutions: the American Revolution and the French Revolution. Lurking behind those revolutions were the English revolutions of the seventeenth century, dedicated, like the American Revolution (but unlike the French Revolution) to constitutional government and the rule of law.

The American Revolution was the transformative event of Hamilton's life, as it was for the other founding fathers and their American contemporaries. In his eyes, the American Revolution had destructive and constructive aspects, both of them welcome and desirable. As a destructive force, the American Revolution shattered British sovereignty over the thirteen mainland colonies of British North America, the jewels in that empire's crown. Not only had the American Revolution ended nearly two centuries of British rule over those colonies; in particular, it broke off the sharp, bitter political dispute over the nature of the unwritten British constitution and its consequences for Americans that had raged between 1765 and 1776. As a constructive force, the American Revolution brought independence, which led to the creation of a new nation, the United States of America. Further, the constructive Revolution spurred more than a decade of state constitution-making, which in turn gave rise to and informed the creation of the US Constitution. Hamilton helped to frame that Constitution, played a pivotal role in its ratification, and was integral to its implementation.

The American Revolution shaped Hamilton's first political writings, in which he explained and defended the Revolutionary cause. That cause led him to enlist in the Continental Army and then to serve for four years as an officer and aide-de-camp to General George Washington. Even after 1783's Treaty of Paris ended the War for Independence, the American Revolution's legacy brought forth Hamilton's greatest efforts as a thinking politician and as a constitutional advocate. Independence and its challenges distilled Hamilton's devotion to the American nation and to its nationalist constitutional vision, both rooted in the American Revolution.

Every other founding father espoused both allegiance to the United States and fealty to one of the American states (such as Massachusetts, New York, or Virginia). Hamilton, however, dedicated himself solely to the independence and development of the American nation. He helped to build that nation by devising a constellation of ideas, principles, institutions, and practices shaped by his nationalism. Even before the United States had won independence, Hamilton shifted from justifying the Revolution to defending its effects. He was arguing for independent American nationhood, melding independence, the Union, and national identity.

For Hamilton, American nationhood included ideals, ideas, and bodies of experience about law and constitutional government that he expounded and defended for the rest of his life. In particular, in the 1780s Hamilton worked to help create a new, effective constitution for the United States. From 1780 to 1785 he sought to help devise an intellectual and political process to frame such a constitution; from 1785 to 1787, he was a leader of the group that drafted that constitution; and from 1787 to 1788, even though he found that constitution's framing frustratingly inadequate, he labored tirelessly to secure the constitution's adoption by the people of the several states. Finally, from 1789 to 1795, as the nation's first secretary of the Treasury, he strove to make the US Constitution an effective form of government for the new nation and to achieve and secure American economic prosperity.

Part of his labors as Treasury Secretary responded to the French Revolution and its effects, both real and perceived. Hamilton was quick to distinguish the American Revolution from the French Revolution. He developed an intense skepticism about the French Revolution. Viewing it with doubt and suspicion, Hamilton could not see in the French Revolution either the American Revolution's links to the rule of law, its deep roots in constitutionalism, or its democratic promise. The French Revolution was not fought on behalf of goals that he could admire, principles that he could share, or methods that he could endorse. Instead, he saw it as a ravening, destructive force threatening Western civilization in the service of what he dismissed as vague, inchoate sentiments of liberty, equality, and brotherhood. Moreover, he saw its effects as destructive to the sound political building central to American constitutionalism.

In sum, Hamilton deemed the French Revolution dangerous. Not only did he think that it had convulsed Europe, threatening security and stability in France, across the Continent, and throughout the Western world. He also worried that ordinary Americans, deluded by the French Revolution's dangerous, leveling brand of politics and government, might unwittingly bring those fearsome tendencies to the United States, where they would wreck and perhaps even destroy the American experiment.

The differences between the revolution that Hamilton saw as founded on law and constitutionalism and the revolution that he saw as threatening law and constitutionalism haunted him. In his understandings of revolution and politics, he could not have differed more from his great adversary Thomas Jefferson. Jefferson did not develop even muted skepticism about the French Revolution until after he became president in 1801. Even so, Jefferson always saw the American and French Revolutions as closely related versions of a common democratic cause; he considered both events as playing central roles in the worldwide age of democratic revolution that he valued so deeply. Jefferson was unmoved by the cautionary lessons that Hamilton absorbed from the French Revolution. So, too, the French Revolution's ideals of liberty, equality, and fraternity, which captivated Jefferson, struck Hamilton as ominous and threatening—because, to him, they were empty words leaving room for violence and chaos. Even so, Hamilton still found inspiration in the idea of independent American nationhood to which the American Revolution gave birth; his commitment to the American national cause was his political and constitutional polestar.

Hamilton first encountered the American Revolution's stirrings in the early 1770s, when he was a student at King's College in New York City, not yet twenty years old and already fascinated by the First Continental Congress (1774). The first intercolonial gathering since the Stamp Act Congress of 1765, the First Continental Congress met at Philadelphia's Carpenters' Hall to coordinate American resistance to British colonial policy. Furthering that purpose, the First Continental Congress adopted an American nonimportation agreement, called the Association, and devised means to enforce it throughout the colonies. The Association's goal was to use an

American boycott of British goods to pressure Britain into recognizing American rights under the unwritten British constitution.

The Association spurred British and Loyalist responses. In particular, in two vigorous pamphlets Rev. Samuel Seabury presented a fully developed Loyalist critique of the First Continental Congress and the Association. Seabury targeted a central colonial argument—the Americans' claim that they were unrepresented in Parliament, which led them to conclude that Parliament had no authority to tax them or otherwise to legislate for them. Instead, Seabury insisted, the Americans had wrongly limited their understanding of representation in Parliament to *actual* representation, ignoring how they were virtually represented in Parliament. Under the theory of virtual representation, Seabury maintained, Parliament's members had the right and the duty to represent all the king's subjects—not just their electoral constituents but all people living in the empire, nonvoting as well as voting. Seabury made this argument the centerpiece of his case against the Americans.

Hamilton refuted Seabury's case for virtual representation and Seabury's advocacy of the rest of the British argument. Three mutually reinforcing ideas formed the core of Hamilton's argument: "we may pronounce it a matter of undeniable certainty, that the pretensions of Parliament are contradictory to the law of nature, subversive of the British constitution, and destructive of the faith of the most solemn compacts."[1] In other words, Hamilton insisted that the American position was true to natural law, to British constitutionalism (as Americans understood it, as a set of restraints on arbitrary power, rather than as an establishment of Parliamentary supremacy), and to the American colonial charters granted by English and British monarchs. In particular, Hamilton invoked ideas of natural law and natural right as ultimate authorities for his position: "The sacred rights of mankind are not to be rummaged for among old parchments or musty records. They are written, as with a sunbeam in the whole volume of human nature, by the hand of the Divinity itself, and can never be erased or obscured by mortal power."[2] Not content with making a defensive case for the colonial position, Hamilton pounded Seabury for bad logic, bogus claims, and disingenuous reasoning. Hamilton thus established his central position in the realm of American political argument.

Turning from fighting words to fighting deeds, Hamilton began working for revolution against Britain. Though some have written that Hamilton left King's College without taking his degree, the college actually closed in the face of the Revolution, leaving Hamilton without a means to finish his collegiate studies. In one of his last actions as a King's College student, he confronted an angry crowd of townsmen who backed the Revolution, addressing them in defense of the college's president, the Loyalist Rev. Myles Cooper; Cooper took advantage of Hamilton's oratory to flee the scene, saving himself from the mob. Expressing his distaste for lawless action, Hamilton was speaking for a Revolution devoted to the rule of law.

Hamilton used the remaining money intended to finance his college education to fund an artillery company, the First New York Artillery. Impressed by his devotion to the cause, New York's Revolutionary leaders named him the artillery company's captain. In mid-1776, he and his company joined the Continental Army's retreat north to New Jersey. Captain Hamilton then led his artillerymen in the critical battles of Trenton and Princeton in December 1776 and January 1777. Distinguishing himself as an intrepid officer, he caught the attention of George Washington, the Continental Army's commander-in-chief; Washington then invited Hamilton to join his staff as an aide-de-camp, with the rank of lieutenant colonel.

For four years, Hamilton was Washington's principal aide, learning how to run an army and administer a war. Maintaining his commitment to the Revolution and to Washington's leadership, he developed his devotion to the cause of an independent American nation. Guiding Hamilton through the Revolution was his fealty to the United States and to American independence. Not only did Hamilton consistently advocate American independence; he argued further for creating a national government as the only

Lt. Col. Alexander Hamilton wears the uniform of the Provincial Company, New York Artillery, during the American War for Independence. *National Archives, War and Conflict 25, NAID: 542435*

form of government appropriate for a new nation. He urged that Americans devise a national government even before the thirteen states had ratified the Articles of Confederation, in 1780 sending a detailed letter on that theme to James Duane, a New York delegate to the Continental Congress. After the Articles' ratification on March 1, 1781, he continued to demand the adoption of a national form of government to replace the rickety Confederation.

Hamilton's espousal of a nationalist vision of America persisted after the American victory won at Yorktown in October 1781, a triumph confirmed by 1783's Treaty of Paris. His advocacy of American constitutional nationalism advanced in tandem with his commitment to American nation-building. In his "Second Letter of Phocion" (1784), published in a New York City newspaper, Hamilton paid eloquent tribute to the Revolution, to its consequences, and to steps that the nation's future demanded:

> The world has its eye upon America. The noble struggle we have made in the cause of liberty has occasioned a kind of revolution in human sentiment. The influence of our example has penetrated the gloomy regions of despotism, and has pointed the way to enquiries which may shake it to its deepest foundations.[3]

Hamilton concluded: "To ripen enquiry into action, it remains for us to justify the revolution by its fruits."[4] His allegiance to that goal inspired his efforts in the Confederation era as a nationalist politician. Those efforts drove him, in the Annapolis Convention in 1786, working with his friend and ally James Madison of Virginia, to get that convention to call for a general constitutional convention. The result was the Federal Convention of 1787. In that body, which framed the proposed US Constitution, Hamilton was a New York delegate, though he was outnumbered and outvoted by the other two New York delegates, Robert Yates and John Lansing Jr., allies of Governor George Clinton who opposed Hamilton's vigorous nationalism. Hamilton had better luck in the ratification controversy of 1787–1788, when he emerged as a leader of those favoring the Constitution's ratification, the Federalists.

Ratification drew Hamilton forward to lead the Federalists in New York; it also spurred him to become an intellectual leader of

Lt. Col. Alexander Hamilton stands with fellow Continental Army officers as the first man at the right, next to the horse, in this lithograph after John Trumbull's painting of the British surrender at the Battle of Yorktown, October 19, 1781. *Library of Congress, LC-DIG-pga-00927*

the pro-Constitution forces. Hamilton advocated the Constitution vigorously and unremittingly. When the delegates in Poughkeepsie finally voted to adopt the Constitution in July 1788, Hamilton won acclaim for his intellectual and political leadership. The cause of the Constitution, he insisted, was the cause of vindicating the American Revolution; adopting the Constitution was the best, perhaps the only, way to preserve the fruits of the Revolution.

Besides his political efforts as a leader of those favoring ratification, Hamilton, with John Jay and James Madison, formed the trio of pro-Constitution polemicists who wrote *The Federalist: or, The New Constitution* (1787–1788), the leading publication arguing for the Constitution in the ratification controversy. Hamilton wrote fifty-one of its eighty-five essays, including classic arguments for national unity, executive power, and judicial review. Valued at the time as a debater's handbook favoring the Constitution, *The Federal-*

ist thereafter won fame as an authoritative case for the Constitution and as the greatest single contribution to American political philosophy and constitutional argument.

After the Constitution's ratification in 1788, Hamilton continued to link American constitutional nationalism with defending the success of the American Revolution. He was especially active during the organization of government under the Constitution, as he prepared himself to become the first secretary of the Treasury in 1789, an office to which he was named by the new nation's first president, George Washington. Hamilton's devotion to constitutional nationalism strengthened during his time in office.

Hamilton's leadership of the Treasury department was the most creative period of his life, intellectually, politically, and constitutionally. Throughout his work as a constitutional advocate and a public administrator, Hamilton championed the Revolution's legacy of an independent American constitutional republic presided over by a national government both energetic and vigorous. His national agenda did not cease with his resignation as Treasury Secretary in January 1795. Afterward, Hamilton was still a Federalist political leader who defined his aims by reference to defending the Constitution and vindicating the American Revolution.

Hamilton's time as Treasury Secretary coincided with the early years of the French Revolution. At its outset, he was taken aback by events in France and recommended wariness as the appropriate American response: "Calculations of what may happen in France must be unusually fallible, not merely from the yet unsettled state of things in that kingdom, but from the extreme violence of the change which has been wrought in the situation of the people."[5] His doubts about France worsened in the 1790s. For example, in February 1794, in the first of his essays written under the pen-name Americanus, Hamilton acknowledged, "There was a time when all men in this country entertained the most favorable view of the French Revolution." And yet, he continued, "None can deny that the cause of France has been stained by excesses and extravagances, for which it is not easy, if possible, to find a parallel in human affairs, and from which reason and humanity recoil." As he argued, observers of events in France "see no where any thing but principles and opinions so wild so extreme passions so turbulent so tempestuous, as almost to forbid the hope of agreement in any rational or well organised system of Government."[6] Throughout the 1790s, and beyond that decade to his death in July 1804, Hamilton combated any prospect that the American nation might fall prey to the seductive political vision of revolutionary France. Profoundly committed to the independent American constitutional republic, bound by the rule of law and dedicated to constitutional politics, he fought to guard the American republic's intellectual and political integrity. Central to his commitment was Hamilton's understanding of American politics.

For most of his adult life, Hamilton was a politician. He was profoundly engaged with politics at two contrasting but complementary levels—that of political theory and that of political practice. Only by understanding both levels of his engagement with politics and the interactions between them can we grasp what kind of politician he was.

Hamilton was a thinking politician, fully engaged with the thrust and parry of actual political combat, while simultaneously immersed in the intellectual dimension of politics, in particular its interaction with constitutionalism and constitutional government. He became and remained a shrewd, able political leader, shaped by his political ideas and beliefs as they evolved over time and also by his ways of practicing politics. He rarely missed a chance to bring those two levels of politics together. He almost never made a pragmatic political argument without juxtaposing it with its intellectual sources, workings, and consequences; he never offered a theoretical argument without addressing its practical sources, dimensions, and results.

Hamilton was fascinated by the theory and practice of constitutional government, and by its foundational ideal of constitutionalism. He saw constitutionalism as a body of ideas and principles empowering as well as limiting government. Thus, his most creative efforts as a thinking politician drove him to explain and to defend the general government's powers under the Constitution, as well as the Constitution's limits on government. This dual commitment made Hamilton perhaps the shrewdest and most creative constitutional theorist and advocate of his time, even as his political positions and constitutional understandings fell outside the consensus shared by most Americans.

Central to Hamilton's vision of constitutionalism were four basic principles—popular sovereignty, energetic government, checks and balances, and federalism. Popular sovereignty, the vision of a form of government created by the American people and responsible to them, was the core of his belief in the necessity and desirability of a republican form of government. He believed that the government of the United States should be republican both because the people of the nation desired republican government and because he himself favored republican government. Energetic government meant for Hamilton a form of government empowered to achieve all those objectives that a government for a republican nation ought to be able to achieve; such a government must be able to define its goals and powers and then use those powers to achieve those goals. Checks and balances stood in Hamilton's view for the contrivances and institutional features that would limit the powers of an otherwise energetic general government to protect republican political principles without impeding that government's ability to achieve its constitutional goals. Federalism stood for another set of ideas and principles: arrangements establishing a constitutional system composed of a powerful but limited federal government side by side with state governments, each with its own powers and limits. Ideally, the federal and state governments would not clash, but if such a clash occurred, the federal government's legitimate powers would prevail over those of a state government.

Hamilton honored his commitment to this framework of constitutional principles throughout his life. They formed the core of his constitutional and political thought. Arguing them with consistency, he was the American politician most invested in and best able to advocate for a vigorous general government and against efforts to limit its powers unduly. His vision of federal constitutional authority was born during the bleakest days of the American Revolution and the most frustrating days of government under the Articles of Confederation. Even in his last years, he clung to his vision of an energetic national constitution empowering a national federal republic.

Of all his writings on constitutionalism, the essays collected in *The Federalist* remain his greatest contributions to political science and constitutional government. Written as part of the national argument for the Constitution in the ratification controversy of 1787–1788, his essays first appeared in New York City's newspapers. The chosen pen name shared by Hamilton, Jay, and Madison was Publius, borrowed from the Roman statesman Publius Valerius Publicola, who led Romans in creating a republican form of government after they had overthrown the city's Etruscan kings. Publius symbolized sound and well-considered political building. And Hamilton's essays written as Publius both argued for and embodied the ideal of sound political building as exemplified by the proposed US Constitution.

Hamilton wrote other series of newspaper essays from the 1780s through the early 1800s—hard-hitting political essays arguing for specific policy goals while anchoring those goals in philosophical and political discussions of constitutional principle. Hamilton was not alone in this tendency to shift from principled disquisition to political combat and back again. Most Federalist and Republican pamphleteers during the early American republic did as he did. The major differences between Hamilton and his contemporaries were, first, the high literary and intellectual quality of his constitutional and political advocacy, and, second, the consistency with which he argued his views.

Hamilton's political methods also were characteristic of his time and far different from the modern practice of democratic politics; in key ways, they were unique to him. Hamilton's approach to politics in substance and style responded to his context. He started as a colonial New Yorker, steeped in New York politics as well as in the intellectual world of the trans-Atlantic Enlightenment. He drew on those bodies of ideas and experience to shape his view of the political problems that he confronted and of the political solutions that he hoped to apply. At the same time that Hamilton responded to his New York setting, however, he also was writing at the beginning of the American Revolution. Thus, even as he debuted as a politician in New York, he also began to craft his chosen role as an American politician. Uniquely free of local political attachments and resentments, he focused on American issues and deployed American strategies and tactics to respond to those issues.

At whatever level we consider Hamilton as a politician, he had a clear set of skills and talents that, taken together, defined his political method. Central to his practice of politics was his crafting and presenting of political arguments in a journalistic setting, via the serial newspaper essay written under a well-chosen pen name. He often picked his pen name to give an added layer of political meaning to his essays. Thus, for example, he used Publius to symbolize sound political building in writing his essays defending the Constitution for *The Federalist*, and he used Pacificus (peace advocate) as the pen name under which he argued for President Washington's authority to proclaim American neutrality in 1793. In this practice, Hamilton was conforming to the common method of eighteenth-century political essayists and pamphleteers.

Hamilton was a quick, energetic polemical writer. So skilled and swift was he in taking up his pen to justify political positions that in the early 1790s Jefferson observed to Madison with more than a touch of envy, "Without numbers he is an host within himself."[7]

The drawback to this virtue was Hamilton's occasional tendency to express himself in extreme, passionate terms overstepping the bounds of controversy, as he did most notoriously in his 1800 pamphlet denouncing the character and conduct of Federalist president John Adams.

Hamilton also had a penchant for personal interaction with fellow politicians who shared his views, which often led him to become chief of his political faction. In that role, Hamilton used a top-down, command-centered approach to politics and political leadership. Though this approach often enabled him to shape and guide his side's approach to political combat, it also was sometimes a disadvantage by comparison with his adversaries' more collegial, less regimented methods. Two linked flaws pervaded his practice of politics, sapping his effectiveness in taking part in political controversy, especially in the late 1790s and early 1800s. The first was Hamilton's self-sabotaging impulsiveness, which often led him to leap into conflict before he had considered carefully what he should argue and how he should argue it. The second was his self-damaging approach to popular politics, which led him to injure his cause, whether by intervening before he was ready to do so or by going to needless extremes in making his case. Again, these faults emerged most often after stepping down in 1795 as Treasury Secretary; it was in that post that he mustered his greatest gifts of effective advocacy and his surest command of linking political arguments to policy goals.

The result of this bundle of skills and faults was an extraordinary period of two dozen years of political activity, from 1780 to 1804. From 1787 to 1795, when he was first New York's leading advocate for the Constitution and then the nation's first Treasury Secretary, he dominated American politics with his extraordinary ability to produce skilled and effective political literature. Time and time again, he defined the American constitutional and political system's central issues and expounded and defended his responses to those issues. In these efforts, he was arguing for a valued cause, independent American nationhood, far more than he was arguing for himself. By contrast, from 1795 to 1804, when he was no longer in public office, he had trouble separating his arguments for a cause from his arguments for himself. At such times, his effectiveness as leader of the Federalist partisan alliance dropped precipitously. By the presidential election of 1800 (which stretched into March 1801), he had wrecked his career as a Federalist political leader—and, in the process, he had helped to sabotage the Federalist cause and to doom the Federalists to irrelevance and disintegration.

After that March, Hamilton had to live with the effects of having shattered his career as a political leader. Though he still practiced politics with his pen, the only avenue left to him, he came to see himself as his former allies saw him—in his own words, as "a disappointed politician."[8] In his last political act, his honor dispute with Aaron Burr in 1804, he was true to his practice of politics while pursuing what we can see as his ultimate self-destructive course. The circumstances surrounding his dispute with Burr, however doomed in retrospect, constituted his sole remaining way to attempt the restoration of his role as a political leader—to risk his life by engaging in a full-blown affair of honor. He was fully aware of the risks that he was taking, and he accepted both those risks and the price that he might have to pay.

Chapter 3

Law and Constitutionalism

More than anyone else in the era of the American founding, Alexander Hamilton was an American nationalist—free of loyalty to any state or local cast of thought, committed solely to an independent American nation. Describing Hamilton as an American nationalist only begins our inquiry, however, for one of the twentieth century's saddest lessons is that there is a spectrum of forms of nationalism, many of them pernicious and dangerous.

What kind of American nationalist was Hamilton? Not only was he dedicated to a vision of a unified, energetic, powerful American nation, but he expressed his nationalist vision through the principles and language of constitutionalism and law. Hamilton saw his nationalism as empowered and limited by law and by its subset, constitutionalism. Ideas and forms of constitutionalism and law defined Hamilton's nationalism, which he used with remarkable consistency and creativity to anchor the development of the American nation, its politics, its economic system, and its place in the world.

Throughout his labors to reform the nation's government and invest it with energy and purpose, Hamilton voiced ideas and made arguments that have continued to shape the development of American constitutional nationalism throughout the nation's history; they are still significant in our own time.

Hamilton based his work as a constitutional nationalist on more than a decade of thinking, writing about, and advocating his vigorous constitutional vision. From his first polemical essays supporting the American cause against Britain in the 1770s, Hamilton was determined to bring into being an independent American nation. Hamilton's essays arguing for independence showed his mastery of the relevant constitutional arguments—first, those powering the dispute between the colonies and the mother country, and then those driving later American struggles to master constitutionalism as a versatile toolkit of nation-building. Hamilton's service as Washington's aide during the War for Independence further instilled in him the need for an energetic national government and the perils of a weak Confederation, confirming his devotion to national constitutional reform. In 1780, he began, while still in the army, to urge leading politicians to replace the Articles of Confederation, which yet awaited ratification by all thirteen states.

After leaving the Continental Army at the end of 1781, and after the French-American victory at the Battle of Yorktown, Hamilton returned to New York City and became a lawyer. His professional self-training continued to enrich his thinking on the evolving national constitutional crisis and the means to bring an effective response to it into being. With energy and determination, he prepared himself to join the New York bar. Most candidates for the bar in the eighteenth century apprenticed themselves to an established practitioner who would supervise their studies, in particular their reading of learned treatises by venerated seventeenth-century jurists such as Sir Edward Coke and Sir Matthew Hale. Hamilton prepared himself for the New York bar without any guidance or help.

The timing of Hamilton's self-preparation was fortuitous. He was among the first American candidates for the bar to have available the greatest English legal treatise, Sir William Blackstone's *Commentaries on the Laws of England* (1765–1769). Hamilton read

Blackstone with pleasure while a young army officer and regularly studied the treatise with care and with interest thereafter. Generations of American lawyers likewise built their legal careers on Blackstone.

Blackstone's *Commentaries,* whose four stout volumes presented the laws of England in a coherent system with elegant clarity, were a revelation to those who were used to English law as set forth in, for example, the gnarled seventeenth-century prose of Sir Edward Coke's *Institutes* and *Reports.* Coke's writings had been the core of law studies for American lawyers such as John Adams, Thomas Jefferson, and John Jay. Those lawyers had to struggle through dense, cryptic texts to assemble their understandings of English law.

Hamilton found in Blackstone's pages a compelling, incisive, and eloquent vision of law as a science—an organized body of knowledge capable of rational analysis, synthesis, and application. That vision had a profound appeal for Blackstone's readers. Blackstone steeped his synthesis of English law in the intellectual spirit of the Age of Enlightenment. What Sir Isaac Newton was to physics and natural philosophy (his era's name for what we call science), what Adam Smith was to moral philosophy and economics, Blackstone was to the law.

Blackstone won Hamilton over; his *Commentaries* formed the basis of Hamilton's law study and legal practice. Just as important, Blackstone furnished Hamilton with a model of argumentative structure and expression. If we were to distill Hamilton's careers as lawyer, constitutional creator, and political advocate into one activity, that activity would be argument. In his own way, like so many other lawyers, Hamilton sought to order the world with words. Blackstone helped to show him how.

A lawyer as great as but significantly different from Hamilton, Jefferson did not share Hamilton's admiration for Blackstone. What dazzled and inspired Hamilton about Blackstone repelled Jefferson. Though he felt grudging respect for Blackstone's intellect and literary grace, Jefferson scorned Blackstone's version of English law as "honeyed Mansfieldism"—"honeyed" because of Blackstone's literary craft; "Mansfieldism" because Jefferson understood Blackstone to echo the great English judge William Murray, Lord Mansfield. To Jefferson, Blackstone, like Mansfield, was an apologist for kingly power and for the British cause during the American Revolution. Jefferson rejected Blackstone's vision of English law as toxic to constitutional liberty.

Unlike Jefferson, Hamilton esteemed Blackstone as an expounder of English law who was essential to Britain's rise as an imperial economic power. As Britain was a model for what Hamilton wanted the United States to become, Britain's law performed for the mother country the functions that, in Hamilton's view, American law should perform in powering the rise of American economic and commercial power. So, too, Hamilton concluded, American constitutionalism should parallel British constitutionalism by creating the doctrinal and institutional framework within which American law would spur the nation's development.

Like any first-rate constitutional thinker, Hamilton knew that constitutionalism stands first for the proposition that, in creating a government, the people both empower and limit their government. As Hamilton recognized, an effective written constitution had to combine empowerment and limitation of the government that its framers sought to create. Hamilton saw the constitutionalism of empowerment not as a merely theoretical goal but as an urgent practical necessity. The United States needed an energetic general government, distinct from the state governments, that would preserve the American nation, its Union, its independence, and its liberties. Under the Articles of Confederation, Americans had no such energetic government. That lack threatened the success of the Revolution, putting at risk the survival of the new nation and of the principles to which it was devoted. Hamilton therefore became an intellectual and political leader of the movement to recognize and remedy the Confederation's fatal defects—to replace the Articles with a new form of government that would empower the United States so that it could truly govern itself.

Hamilton built up a thriving practice within two years of his admission to the New York bar in 1782. In the process, he wove together his legal skills with his commitment to constitutional reform in the national interest. In 1784, for example, Hamilton took a case having important consequences for the interaction after the Revolution among New York law, national interests and concerns, and the law of nations. The focal point of this interaction was the Treaty of Paris of 1783, which ended the War for Independence. The issue was the control of a New York brewery by British occupation forces during the war.

In *Rutgers v. Waddington,* Elizabeth Rutgers, the brewery's owner, sued Josiah Waddington, a merchant who had operated her brewery during the British occupation. Mrs. Rutgers sought damages for Waddington's allegedly illegal running of the brewery. As the basis of her lawsuit, she invoked New York's Trespass Act of 1783, a statute enacted after the war that gave plaintiffs like Mrs. Rutgers a cause of action against men like Waddington for deeds that they had committed under authority granted by British occupation forces but which, plaintiffs argued, deprived them of their legal rights. Mrs. Rutgers ignored the 1783 Treaty of Paris, which in Hamilton's view the New York statute violated. Waddington claimed protection from Mrs. Rutgers's lawsuit under two licenses that, he claimed, allowed him to operate the brewery. The first had been issued by the British commissary general; the second had been issued by the commander of the British forces occupying New York City.

In advocating for Waddington, Hamilton invoked the law of nations. He insisted that the British commander's license gave Waddington the right to operate the brewery under the law of nations and the Treaty of Paris, despite New York's Trespass Act. In essence, Hamilton argued that the 1783 Treaty of Paris, an American treaty binding the United States and the several states to peace with Great

Britain, included the law of nations and thus limited the operation of New York law, specifically the state's Trespass Act. Presiding over the Mayor's Court of the City of New York, Mayor James Duane accepted Hamilton's argument; he granted Mrs. Rutgers damages only for the short time when Waddington operated the brewery under his license from the British commissary-general but not for the time that Waddington invoked the authority of the British commander's license. The Mayor's Court based its decision on the law of nations as construed by Hamilton's argument for Waddington. Thus, Duane held, the Treaty of Paris of 1783 and the law of nations outranked the New York statute—a victory for national supremacy.

Two years later, Hamilton struck a blow for national constitutional reform. In September 1786, as a New York delegate to the Annapolis Convention, a body considering proposing reform of the Articles of Confederation's regulation of commerce, he wrote (with the support of James Madison, a Virginia delegate) the convention's report to the Confederation Congress and the several states. That report proposed a general convention to meet in Philadelphia in May 1787 to render the constitution of American government "adequate to the exigencies of the Union."[1] Before Hamilton acted, the Annapolis Convention appeared doomed to failure; afterward, Hamilton's report salvaged the Annapolis Convention and redefined the agenda of American politics to put American constitutional reform at its core.

In 1786 and 1787, every state except Rhode Island appointed delegates to the Federal Convention. Half the states followed the guidance of the Annapolis Convention's report; the other states followed the resolution adopted on February 21, 1787, by the Confederation Congress, which responded to the Annapolis Convention while differing slightly from its reasoning. New York's legislature named Hamilton one of the state's three delegates to the Convention. When he and his colleagues got to Philadelphia, however, Hamilton felt growing frustration, even though he had worked hard to bring the Convention into being. His fellow New York delegates,

Robert Yates and John Lansing Jr., outvoted him in the Convention on every major issue. Committed to their alliance with New York's governor, George Clinton, Yates and Lansing were, like Clinton, content with New York's advantageous position as a wealthy and powerful state in a fragile Confederation; thus, they saw no need for constitutional change. Further, even such allies as Madison would not go as far as Hamilton thought was needed to devise a strong national government.

On June 18, 1787, Hamilton finally gave voice to his frustration. In an epic speech, he derided the Articles and dismissed as inadequate the two leading proposals offered to replace them. Instead, he offered his own idea of a radically national form of government with sweeping powers to regulate commerce and taxation, reducing the states to administrative districts, with their governors appointed by the national chief executive. Many admired his oratory—but none backed his plan.[2]

In July, disappointed by his failure to persuade the other Convention delegates, Hamilton left the Convention to resume his law practice in New York; he was convinced that there was no point to staying in Philadelphia. Yates and Lansing also left for home around the same time; they recognized their failure to persuade their fellow delegates to reject a new form of government for the United States and decided to return to New York to report their failure to Governor Clinton. In September, however, Hamilton returned to the Convention for its last few weeks of debate. He capped his time as a Convention delegate on September 17 by speaking in favor of the proposed Constitution. He also signed the Constitution on behalf of New York, even though, as only one of the state's three delegates, he did not have the power to commit his state. As he said, no man's ideas were further from the plan than his were known to be, but the chance of good to be expected from the Constitution was better than the chaos that would come without it.

Days after the Convention's end, Hamilton prepared a memorandum, "Conjectures on the New Constitution," in which he predicted that the Constitution might fail to win ratification, or that it might fail even if it was ratified.[3] He also foretold with uncanny accuracy that the Constitution's fate in the ratification controversy would be decided within nine or ten months of the Convention's end. Despite this memorandum, and in the face of his doubts about the Constitution's future, he determined to give the proposed Constitution the best chance that it could have in the ratification controversy.

Hamilton became the leader of pro-Constitution forces in New York, working with such allies as John Jay and Robert R. Livingston. Elected to the New York ratifying convention, he was only one of nineteen pro-Constitution delegates, or Federalists, facing forty-six delegates opposing the Constitution, or Anti-Federalists. In their grim determination and mastery of the arts of constitutional and political argument, however, the Federalists were a match for their adversaries. Insisting on clause-by-clause debate of the Constitution, Hamilton led the Federalists on the convention floor, while Jay worked behind the scenes to win over wavering Anti-Federal delegates. Meanwhile, the Federalists waited for favorable news from the ratifying conventions of Virginia and New Hampshire. By June 1788, eight states had already ratified the Constitution, and none had rejected it. As three state ratifying conventions were meeting simultaneously that month in New York, New Hampshire, and Virginia, June 1788 witnessed the ordeal of the Constitution; any one state's ratification would mean that the Constitution would be the new form of government for the ratifying states. Within weeks, news of ratifications by New Hampshire and Virginia arrived in Poughkeepsie, carried by express riders paid for by Hamilton. In the wake of the news of those state ratifications, New York's Anti-Federalists had to rethink their position. Ten states, one more than the ratification procedure of Article VII required, had voted to ratify the Constitution. Now the New York delegates' choice was radically different: either they could vote to join the Union by ratifying the Constitution or they could vote to leave the Union by rejecting it. After days of debate, enough Anti-Federalists (led by their floor leader, Melancton Smith) abandoned the fight against the Constitution, joining with Hamilton, Jay, and the Federalists to ratify it, by a vote of 30–27.

At the same time that he was leading New York's Federalists during the ratification convention, Hamilton launched a distinctly eighteenth-century political venture: a series of newspaper essays, which he wrote with Jay and Madison, to make the case for adopting the Constitution. They titled the essay series *The Federalist; or, The New Constitution*; their shared pen name was Publius, from the Roman statesman Publius Valerius Publicola ("people-lover"), who led the founding of Rome's republican government after the Romans had overthrown their Etruscan kings. The name Publius symbolized sound political building, a value that the authors of *The Federalist* sought to associate with the cause of the new Constitution.

That so enduring a work of constitutional advocacy began as a twice-weekly newspaper column is remarkable. Despite the speed with which they wrote, *The Federalist* is a commanding work of political argument, combining theory and practice, principle and reality. In some essays, Hamilton predicted how the Constitution would work based on his experience of how the Confederation had and had not worked. Some of his predictions failed to come true—but, on his central themes of constitutional government, Hamilton's essays were sound and prophetic.

For example, after a memorable demolition of the Articles of Confederation (in *The Federalist* Nos. 15–22), Hamilton did his most creative work as Publius in defending the new national executive and judiciary—institutions that the Confederation did not have but that the system created by the Constitution needed to work. Americans distrusted executive and judicial power because of their abuses by English kings and colonial royal governors and judges. Hamilton had to disprove that conventional wisdom, to show that the presidency and the federal courts were necessary and desirable parts of a fully worked-out national constitutional system.

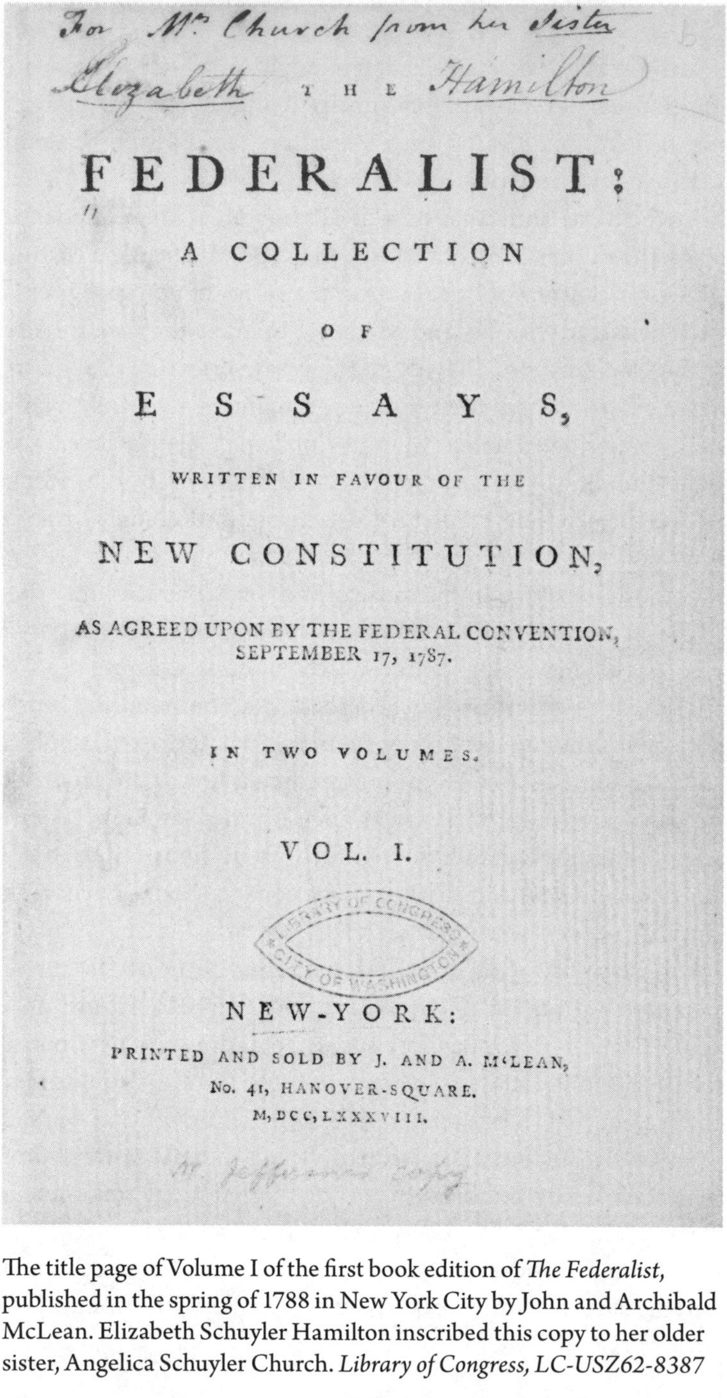

For Mrs Church from her Sister
Elizabeth Hamilton

THE

FEDERALIST:

A COLLECTION

OF

ESSAYS,

WRITTEN IN FAVOUR OF THE

NEW CONSTITUTION,

AS AGREED UPON BY THE FEDERAL CONVENTION,
SEPTEMBER 17, 1787.

IN TWO VOLUMES.

VOL. I.

NEW-YORK:

PRINTED AND SOLD BY J. AND A. M'LEAN,
No. 41, HANOVER-SQUARE.
M,DCC,LXXXVIII.

Mr. Jefferson's Copy

The title page of Volume I of the first book edition of *The Federalist,* published in the spring of 1788 in New York City by John and Archibald McLean. Elizabeth Schuyler Hamilton inscribed this copy to her older sister, Angelica Schuyler Church. *Library of Congress, LC-USZ62-8387*

In *The Federalist* Nos. 69 and 70, Hamilton rejected the idea that the presidency would be what Edmund Randolph of Virginia had denounced in the Federal Convention as the "foetus of monarchy." Rather, he insisted, executive power was necessary, because executive functions are necessary to any sound government. Necessary functions implied a necessary institution wielding necessary powers to carry out those functions. Further, Hamilton wrote, a one-person chief executive would be both more effective and more accountable than either a plural chief executive or a one-man chief executive exercising powers with an advisory council. Hamilton was an enthusiast for executive power; even so, he also defended the concept of political responsibility as a constitutional value and applied it to the presidency. As Hamilton argued, making the president one person would make it easier to hold him responsible for his actions. Hamilton also pointed out that, unlike the British king, whose person "is sacred and inviolable," the nation could hold the president to a standard of personal responsibility like that binding the governor of a state and could use the power of impeachment, built into the Constitution's text (with deep roots in English and American colonial history), to check a president seeking to abuse his powers.[4]

Hamilton took a similar approach to explaining and defending the new federal judicial institutions to be created under the Constitution's Article III. In *The Federalist* Nos. 78–83,[5] Hamilton defused American fears of federal courts. Instead, Hamilton showed that federal judges would not have unlimited power (lest they seem dangerous), nor that they would have no power or purpose (lest they seem unnecessary). Rather, he demonstrated that they would play a vital role in constitutional government. Rejecting charges that federal courts would run amok, he insisted that federal judges would wield only a text-bound power to interpret the Constitution and laws of the United States, and that they would have power to act only in actual disputes ("cases and controversies") coming before them. He showed further that the judiciary would have the key responsibility and power—what we call judicial review—to interpret the Constitution to protect it from statutes or executive actions violating its limits on power; the courts would not allow the extension of federal power beyond what the Constitution allowed.

Hamilton distinguished between two kinds of judicial review. One was coequal or federal/federal judicial review (a federal court reviewing a federal statute or government action by reference to the Constitution). The other was supervisory or federal/state judicial review (a federal court reviewing a state statute or government action by reference to the Constitution). Supervisory judicial review, having a textual root in the Constitution (the supremacy clause of Article VI), was easy to defend. To justify coequal judicial review, Hamilton stressed the difference between ordinary laws (or ordinary government actions having force of law) and fundamental law (the US Constitution), the latter made by the People of the United States exercising their constituent power—the power to constitute a government. Fundamental law, he concluded, must prevail over ordinary statute law or government actions.

To drive his point home, Hamilton invoked the law of agency, a familiar component of Anglo-American common law. As the principal's will prevails over an agent's unauthorized actions, because actions exceeding the principal's will fall outside the agent's granted authority, so the Supreme Court has the power and the duty to defend the Constitution against unauthorized acts by Congress or the executive, for those acts exceed the authority granted government institutions by the People of the United States through the Constitution.

The Federalist helped both its readers and its authors to refocus their thinking about politics, government, and law within the matrix of the Constitution. The essays strengthened Hamilton's commitment to energetic nationalism expressed by constitutional means. With Blackstone's *Commentaries*, it became a foundation for Hamilton's later efforts of constitutional interpretation.

Though the Constitution, ratified in 1788, established the new form of government of the United States in 1789, that victory did not end the controversy over the Constitution, for neither framing nor ratification ended the process of constitution-making. The new national charter had to be put into effect—a task as difficult and dangerous as its framing and ratification had been—and Hamilton was integral to that process. In September 1789, President Washington named Hamilton the nation's first secretary of the Treasury. The federal statute creating the office, which Hamilton had helped to frame behind the scenes, barred the secretary from handling the nation's money but required him to make public policy and to run the Treasury department, including preparing reports on the public credit when Congress asked him to do so. Congress saw that responsibility as limiting the secretary's discretion, but Hamilton saw it as a way to enable him to set the national political agenda.

Hamilton's reports outlined a bold plan. The first report proposed that the federal government assume state debts from the Revolution, consolidate them with the Confederation's existing debts, and devise a policy for their gradual repayment, while using them to spur economic growth. Hamilton's assumption plan touched off a constitutional crisis leading to the Compromise of 1790, in which Secretary of State Thomas Jefferson acted as an honest broker between Hamilton and Madison, who as the leading member of the House of Representatives had been the most powerful foe of Hamilton's assumption plan.

Not until he confronted the next step of Hamilton's policy—the December 1790 report proposing the creation of a national bank to manage the consolidated debt and otherwise oversee the nation's finances—did Jefferson discern what he denounced as Hamilton's centralizing, corrupting policy. To Jefferson, that policy came unnervingly close to Great Britain's fiscal system built around the Bank of England, which Jefferson saw as corrupting British government.

What the Assumption bill began, the Bank bill accelerated—helping to split the nation into two great partisan alliances, Federalists and Republicans. The Federalists of the 1790s championed a strong, energetic federal government; the Republicans proclaimed their commitment to limited federal government that embodied republican principles that opposed corruption. After vigorous debate, Congress enacted the Bank bill, but the measure faced a roadblock in the executive branch. Rep. Madison, a leading advisor to President Washington, joined with two leading members of the cabinet—Secretary of State Jefferson and Attorney General Edmund Randolph—to challenge the bill's constitutionality. They argued that the Bank bill was invalid because the Constitution did not explicitly give Congress the power to charter a bank. Jefferson and Randolph submitted written opinions to Washington against the Bank bill's constitutionality, and Madison began to draft a veto message for the president. Troubled, Washington gave Jefferson's and Randolph's opinions to Hamilton, asking him to answer them if he could.

Neither side in this dispute was heroic or villainous. Rather, Federalists and Republicans held sincere, conflicting visions of what the American nation was and should be. Constitutional argument is about more than the Constitution—it is about competing visions of the American nation that crystallize as arguments about how to interpret the Constitution.

Jefferson's vision of America (shared by Madison and Randolph, though not with Jefferson's ardor) drew on his idealized conception of his native Virginia and his firsthand knowledge of the Old World's corruption and decadence. Jefferson saw the United States as a self-sufficient nation of yeoman farmers who worked to produce only what they needed to support themselves and who disdained the luxuries of European consumer goods. Jefferson's America needed only a wise, frugal federal government with limited powers. The people of the several states, allied by shared interests and commitments to one another and to their vision of the Revolution, would not need an energetic national government supreme over the states to preserve that Union. In fact, Jefferson thought, an energetic national government that wielded broad powers would be an engine of corruption that would undermine the virtue needed to sustain the good society; it would bring a corrupt monarchy and aristocracy that would destroy the fruits of the Revolution.

On public policy and on constitutional doctrine, Hamilton's differences with Jefferson were stark. Where Jefferson wanted America to hold Europe at arm's length, Hamilton wanted America to engage fully and profitably in the world's commercial network; he insisted that the United States could not and should not seal itself off from the world. Hamilton hoped to call into being a diverse national economy, with agriculture, commerce, and manufacturing supporting one another like the legs of a three-legged stool. The result would be an independent, wealthy, powerful nation of equal standing with any great European power, proof against the threat of European interference. Hamilton's experiences of American weakness under the Articles of Confederation pushed his thinking in a direction opposed to Jefferson's views. In *The Federalist* No. 85, Hamilton had declared that "A NATION without a NATIONAL GOVERNMENT is, in my view, an awful spectacle."[6] Hamilton maintained that too many sources of antagonism among the states would erode the shared commitments to preserve the Union in which Jefferson put his faith. Throughout *The Federalist,* Hamilton warned of threats of civil war at home and invasion from abroad; he cautioned that both kinds of threats would be exacerbated by a weak general government unable to defend the Union or to vindicate its interests.

In February 1791, when his intellectual clash with Jefferson was sharpest and most direct, Hamilton saw the task before him—justifying the Bank bill as constitutional—as clear and urgent. Within a week, he prepared his "Opinion on the Constitutionality of a National Bank" and delivered it to the president.[7] After reading and being persuaded by Hamilton's opinion, Washington signed the Bank bill into law, ending the specific dispute between his advisors but not the larger argument. To this day, the contest between Hamilton and Jefferson over the Bank bill defines the poles of argument over constitutional interpretation between two ways of interpreting the Constitution's language, restrictive versus generous constitutional interpretation.

Hamilton focused on the issue of federal power under the Constitution. Did the Constitution grant only those powers explicitly mentioned in its text, and did its "necessary and proper" clause authorize only powers truly "necessary," with the word "proper" meaning only constitutional? So Jefferson maintained, but Hamilton disagreed; he made a powerful case for reading the Constitution broadly to confer both explicitly mentioned powers and a wide category of other powers deducible from and related to explicit powers—implied powers. Only if the Constitution specifically banned a given power, Hamilton argued, was that power out of bounds. He made this point over and over again, from many different angles, but he always kept his central purpose in view—to expound and justify a broad reading of the Constitution and of the powers that it conferred on the federal government, express and implied, including the power to charter a bank. Both express powers implying other powers not prohibited and express purposes implying other powers not prohibited combined to define the outer limits of implied powers, Hamilton taught. Thus, he maintained, the Constitution did not confer open-ended grants of all sorts of powers, but only those implied powers clearly linked to express grants of power or to express constitutional statements of purposes for which the Constitution granted power.

Arguments over constitutional interpretation moved beyond the debate on express versus implied powers to invade other spheres of constitutional authority. As the 1790s unfolded, for example, issues of foreign policy interacted with issues of national interests and with the constitutional system. The causes were the French Revolution of 1789, the resulting war pitting revolutionary

France against the monarchies of Europe led by Great Britain, and the question of whether that war could embroil the United States. France had had a treaty of alliance with the new nation since 1778, but that treaty was with the French monarchy, not with the revolutionary French republic. Could France now invoke the old treaty to drag the United States into a European war, or could the United States cite the French change of government as reason to proclaim its neutrality despite the treaty? Those questions in turn raised the issue of who in the federal government, Congress or the president, had the authority to make that policy decision on American neutrality under the Constitution.

Hamilton emerged as an advocate of executive authority and discretion; he hoped to give President Washington as much power as he needed to steer the United States through the crisis. Hamilton prevailed in a cabinet meeting, persuading all except Jefferson that

This engraving by Cornelius Tiebout shows the first capitol of the United States, Federal Hall in New York City, where Treasury Secretary Hamilton regularly met with members of the First Federal Congress in 1789–90. *Library of Congress, LC-USZ62-2566*

the change in France's government relieved the United States of obligations to France under the 1778 treaty. Then he knew that he had to make his case in the court of public opinion.

Hamilton's usual approach to such issues was, as with *The Federalist*, to write a series of powerful newspaper essays blending constitutional argument, policy analysis, and partisan polemic. He wrote as Pacificus to defend the president's authority to proclaim the nation's neutrality between revolutionary France and the coalition of conservative European monarchies led by Great Britain. In a formidable forensic duel, Hamilton and Madison (who wrote as Helvidius) laid out the lines of debate on executive versus congressional authority over foreign policy that still shape the issue. In the 1790s, Hamilton's arguments prevailed.

For the rest of his life, Hamilton remained engaged with the Constitution and his vision of the government that it authorized. Always he argued for a broad, generous interpretation of federal constitutional power as essential to preserve the Union and to protect American interests at home and abroad. Within that context, he argued to defend executive power in the constitutional system. In the process, he was reviled by his enemies and buffeted by controversy, much of it of his own making. In 1802, he wrote sadly to an old friend and ally, Gouverneur Morris, "Mine is an odd destiny. Perhaps no man in the United States has sacrificed or done more for the present Constitution than myself. And, contrary to all my expectations, I still have to work to prop up its frail and worthless fabric. For my reward, I have a few murmurs from its friends and loud curses from its enemies. The best thing I can do is withdraw from the scene. Every day proves to me more and more that this American world is not made for me."[8] Hamilton died holding these views, never imagining that the Constitution would fulfill his hopes for vindicating American national interests.

It is almost impossible to separate arguments about the Constitution and its meaning from those who made the arguments. The problem is not that we keep both levels of meaning in mind, but rather that we too often fail to keep the line separating them in mind. Too many people who write about this period take sides, for or against Hamilton, Adams, Jefferson, or Madison. This tendency is natural, but dangerous nonetheless. Works of history or constitutional argument should not wear metaphorical campaign buttons on their lapels. Rather, the American experiment needed all of these people—the first-rank founding fathers, the middle-rank politicians and printers who acted as conduits and buffers between them and the great body of the people, and the people themselves. These interactions among all of them, often bitter and contentious, helped to shape the American constitutional experiment, the American political and legal systems, and the fate of the American Revolution. Only by understanding their heated, intricate arguments about the American constitutional experiment and the reasons that they made those arguments can we understand the anchoring of American law, the evolution of American constitutionalism, and the pivotal roles that Alexander Hamilton played and still plays in those controversies.

Chapter 4

Political Economy and Public Administration

Political economy and public administration occupied the center of Alexander Hamilton's political, economic, and constitutional vision. The centrality of those two constellations of ideas shaped his approach to serving as the nation's first secretary of the Treasury; in turn, they profoundly influenced the new nation's emerging public policy, economic policy, and political evolution. For these reasons, his understandings of those subjects made his service as Treasury Secretary pivotal to the launch of government and politics under the US Constitution.

Hamilton was no economic ideologue; his goal was not to argue for pure or abstract economic theories, but rather to nourish the economic growth of the United States and to promote the federal government's strength and integrity. What linked those great goals for him were economic policies consistent with the new nation's Constitution and laws. Although he studied such leading works of economic thought as *On the Wealth of Nations* by Adam Smith, he did not seek to expound these works' theoretical models of economics. Rather, he sought to put ideas about economics to work to meet practical economic and political goals. For him, the realms of economics and public policy were congruent. For him, sound economic advocacy and sound political argument were joined at the hip.

Nor was Hamilton the only leading American whose guiding ideas blended economic and political principles. Jefferson also advocated what he saw as sensible economic policy wedded to an equally sensible political vision of what America should be. The question facing Hamilton and Jefferson was which of their visions would prevail, and which in turn would define the nation's future. Each man saw the conflict between those constellations of ideas and principles as having vital consequences for the development of the American economy, for the roles and responsibilities of the nation's constitutional system relevant to economic matters, and for the future of the American people.

In the realm of public policymaking, Hamilton saw the need to develop in tandem the nation's prosperity and the health of its government, both of which would prosper under his supervision. He sought to promote a unified economy that blended three equally strong components—agriculture, commerce, and manufacturing. This economic model differed starkly from Jefferson's hopes for an agrarian economy embodying the labor of thrifty, self-sufficient yeoman farmers.

Together with his policy goals, Hamilton sought to develop his day-to-day mastery of running the Treasury department. To achieve that goal, he recognized the need to formulate and apply methods of public administration. Hamilton saw public administration as an indispensable supplement to making public policy; it was the means by which he could make the Treasury department do its work. Further, he recognized that well-reasoned public policy fitted together with well-reasoned public administration to create the vital foundation to undergird sensible American political economy.

As he contemplated the relationship between government and the economy, Hamilton stressed the prudent, targeted use of federal government power; he hoped to use that power to promote economic growth and diversification. Hamilton's understanding of economics and his understanding's resonance with constitutional nationalism showed him what he deemed to be the best means to foster constructive interaction among national, political, and economic development. He designed his strategic approach to reshaping the national economy so that he could make it competitive with the economies of such great powers as Great Britain. His ultimate goal was to establish the United States as a rising power in the world economy.

Throughout his career, Hamilton pursued his vision of an energetic, mixed American economy poised to achieve a commanding role in the world. Critical to the difference between his economic worldview and Jefferson's (and Madison's) agrarian economic vision was that Jefferson and Madison had economic roots in and political commitments to agrarian Virginia, and their roots and commitments shaped and expressed their economic ideas. By contrast, Hamilton owed his economic and political allegiance solely to the United States and thus to its multifaceted economy.

Hamilton extolled the greatness of each element of the mixed economy as he saw it, while urging as well that the nation nurture the necessary relationships among them. Hamilton preserved the consistency of his economic vision, as well as his grasp of the linkages that sustained it, bolstered his constitutional goals, and fueled his political activism. At the same time, in response to the weakness of the nation's economy in the 1780s, he worked tirelessly to establish its fiscal health once he occupied the office of Treasury Secretary. Hamilton saw the economy's health as interwoven with that of the federal government. Hamilton acknowledged the necessity for bold advocacy of his vision of a complex American political economy complementing his conception of an active and vigorous national government that was committed to the development of that economy.

Hamilton focused on thinking through his responsibilities as Treasury Secretary, using his political and economic ideas to give effect to both. In particular, he worked to use the federal government to promote national fiscal security and economic growth. As Treasury Secretary, he focused on the interactions among finance, economics, and government and on the best ways to use those interactions to nourish the American economy and to strengthen the American nation-state. Hamilton saw that the nation and its economy had to grow and develop together.

Hamilton's focus on political economy was integral to his philosophy of government—his views of what government should achieve, what ends it should serve, and what benefits it should generate and for whom. Hamilton argued that an American economy devoted solely to agriculture would leave that country too dependent on foreign nations and thus unable to support itself, though he acknowledged the value of agriculture and its centrality to American economic life. A national economy, he maintained, had to use such political and legal mechanisms as tariffs (taxes on products imported from overseas producers) and bounties (government payments to encourage economic actors to take constructive economic steps) to protect local industries. (He did not, however, favor raising tariffs so prohibitively high as to exclude competing imports.) Hamilton thus did not espouse a purely free-trade economy or a purely protectionist economy. Instead, he favored modest, judicious use of tariffs and of bounties to give domestic products an advantageous economic position that would make them competitive with imports.

Hamilton wrote reports to Congress on what he called "the public credit" to identify and to advocate his goals for the American economy and to make the case for his economic and political agenda. He benefited from Congress's decision in 1789 to obligate the Treasury Secretary to submit such reports to it. Congress saw such reports as means to keep the Treasury Secretary under congressional supervision; by contrast, Hamilton saw the writing of such reports as an expansion of his official power and discretion. He recognized that the writing of such reports would empower him to set the nation's domestic fiscal and political agenda.

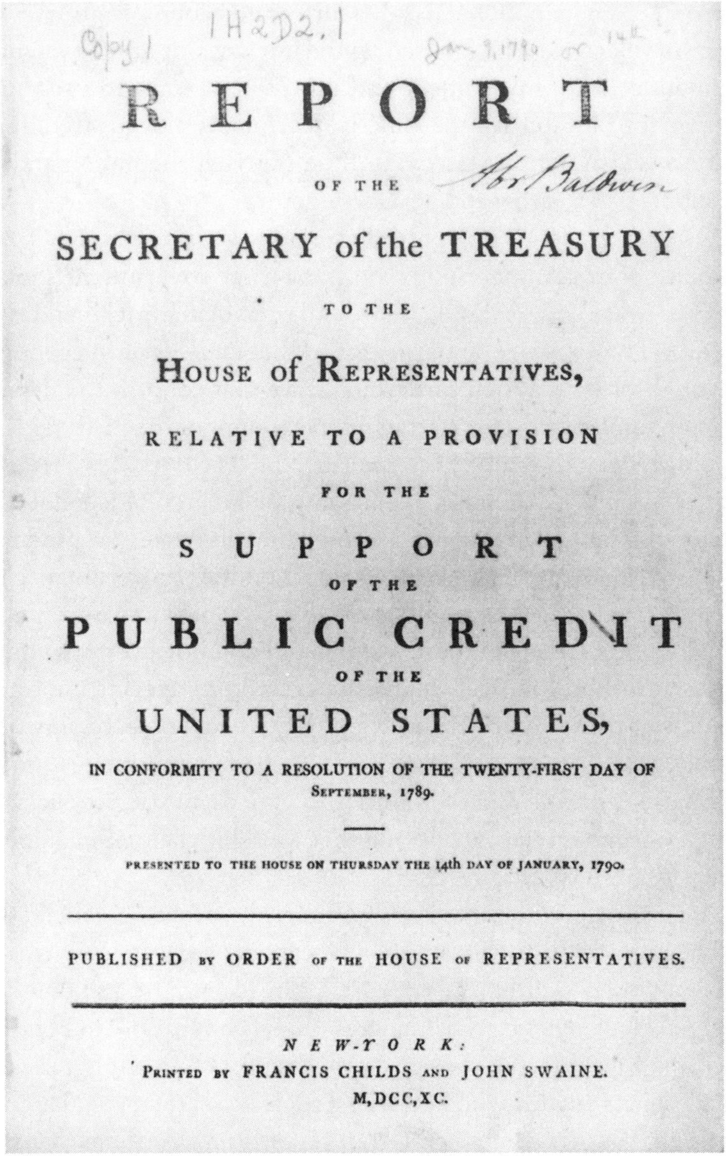

REPORT

OF THE

SECRETARY of the TREASURY

TO THE

HOUSE of REPRESENTATIVES,

RELATIVE TO A PROVISION

FOR THE

SUPPORT

OF THE

PUBLIC CREDIT

OF THE

UNITED STATES,

IN CONFORMITY TO A RESOLUTION OF THE TWENTY-FIRST DAY OF SEPTEMBER, 1789.

PRESENTED TO THE HOUSE ON THURSDAY THE 14th DAY OF JANUARY, 1790.

PUBLISHED BY ORDER OF THE HOUSE OF REPRESENTATIVES.

NEW-YORK:
PRINTED BY FRANCIS CHILDS AND JOHN SWAINE.
M,DCC,XC.

As Treasury Secretary, Hamilton submitted his first *Report on the Public Credit* to the First Federal Congress on January 9, 1790. This report laid the foundation for his financial program for the new nation. *Library of Congress, LC-USZ62-60769*

Hamilton's first report was his *Report Relative to a Provision for the Support of Public Credit,* which he submitted to Congress on January 9, 1790. In the fall of 1789, a committee of merchants in Philadelphia had sent to Congress their demand that the federal government preserve the American nation's public credit, specifically seeking payment of the nation's public debts. A House committee led by Rep. James Madison referred the merchants' demand to Hamilton, who at once set to work. As he was finishing his report, he confessed to his wife's older sister Angelica Schuyler Church that he was "very busy and not a little anxious."[1] Fueling himself with cup after cup of black coffee, he finished his work in time to submit his report to Congress at the start of its second session.[2]

Members of Congress found Hamilton's long yet vigorous report astonishing. In it, he defined the first stage of his program as Treasury Secretary: to take the measure of the debt of the United States (much of it owed to foreign creditors) plus the debts of the several states, and to devise a plan for the federal government to respond to this challenge. Some states, chiefly in the South, had taken extensive steps to repay and liquidate their debts; others, chiefly in the North, had not done so. Further, because the states used different currencies, the result was a near-chaotic financial conundrum for anyone seeking to untangle the mess, let alone respond to it. Such was the gargantuan problem facing Hamilton, who also had to grapple with the web of confused suspicion that inevitably gathered around any finance minister. For decades, finance ministers in European governments had faced suspicion and hostility as they struggled to maintain structures of public finance against charges of corruption; Hamilton knew that he would face similar charges from his political foes. Fortunately, Hamilton never let the array of difficulties that he faced intimidate him.

Hamilton proposed that the federal government assume the United States' debts left over from the Revolution, and the states' debts, and consolidate all of these obligations into one great package of debt owed by the federal government on behalf of the

United States. Then the federal government would begin to work out a way of gradual repayment of the nation's amassed debt. The nation would repay the foreign debt in full to bolster its credit in the world economy. The government would also retire the consolidated states' debts over time, creating a fund to do so—a continuing obligation to which the government would devote a set portion of the national revenue each year to retire interest and part of the principal. By shifting the states' debts to the federal government, Hamilton argued, there would be less competition for tax revenue between the states and the federal government. The balance of the debt would be the basis for issuing public securities, which would expand the national supply of circulating currency. That increase in turn would help spur a national economic recovery.

Response to Hamilton's first report divided the nation; some criticized what they saw as Hamilton's favoritism for the rich and for the Northern states. Controversy raged, until the negotiation of what became the Compromise of 1790. In that compromise, agreed to by Hamilton and Madison with Jefferson, Madison relaxed his opposition and allowed two Virginians in the House to support Hamilton's plan, in exchange for which the nation's capital would be moved from New York to Philadelphia for ten years, and then to a permanent location on the banks of the Potomac River between Virginia and Maryland.

Hamilton's second report, the *Report on a National Bank,* which defined the second stage of his program. reached Congress on December 13, 1790.[3] This report was as incisive, sophisticated, and daring as his first. In it, Hamilton proposed the creation of a semi-private Bank of the United States, which would receive deposits of federal tax revenues, act as a storehouse for those funds, manage the government's finances, and help to provide the United States with a stable circulating medium of exchange—a national currency. Having learned from the example of Great Britain's Bank of England, Hamilton proposed that the Bank of the United States become its American counterpart. After stormy and passionate debate, accompanied by bitter public controversy, Congress enacted the bill creating the Bank and sent it to President Washington for his signature. This time, however, Hamilton faced united opposition from the Virginians in Washington's cabinet: Secretary of State Jefferson and Attorney General Edmund Randolph, as well as Rep. Madison. Their argument was that the Constitution had no provision authorizing Congress to create a bank; therefore, the bill passed by Congress was unconstitutional and Washington should veto it. Jefferson argued that the Constitution should be interpreted strictly, with no room for extending its powers by interpretation or implication, and Randolph agreed. Troubled by Jefferson's and Randolph's written opinions against the Bank bill, Washington referred them and the bill to Hamilton, asking him to justify the bill if he could. Meanwhile, he asked Madison to draft a veto message.

Writing swiftly, within a week Hamilton had ready his "Opinion on the Constitutionality of a National Bank."[4] At its core, Hamilton put an argument that was the reverse of Jefferson's. Hamilton proposed to read the Constitution broadly. Whereas Jefferson demanded an explicit constitutional provision authorizing an action by Congress such as the Bank bill, Hamilton responded that Congress could enact such a bill so long as it was in pursuance of a constitutional objective and the Constitution had no provision that barred Congress from enacting such a bill. Hamilton also noted various provisions of the Constitution setting forth purposes for which the Bank bill was relevant. Given that there were constitutional purposes that the bill would answer and no constitutional prohibition on such a bill, Hamilton concluded that the Bank bill was constitutional and that Washington could sign it into law. Persuaded by Hamilton's reasoning, Washington signed the Bank bill. In their epic argument over the constitutionality of the Bank bill, Hamilton and Jefferson established one of the great enduring constitutional disputes—that between broad and strict constitutional interpretation.

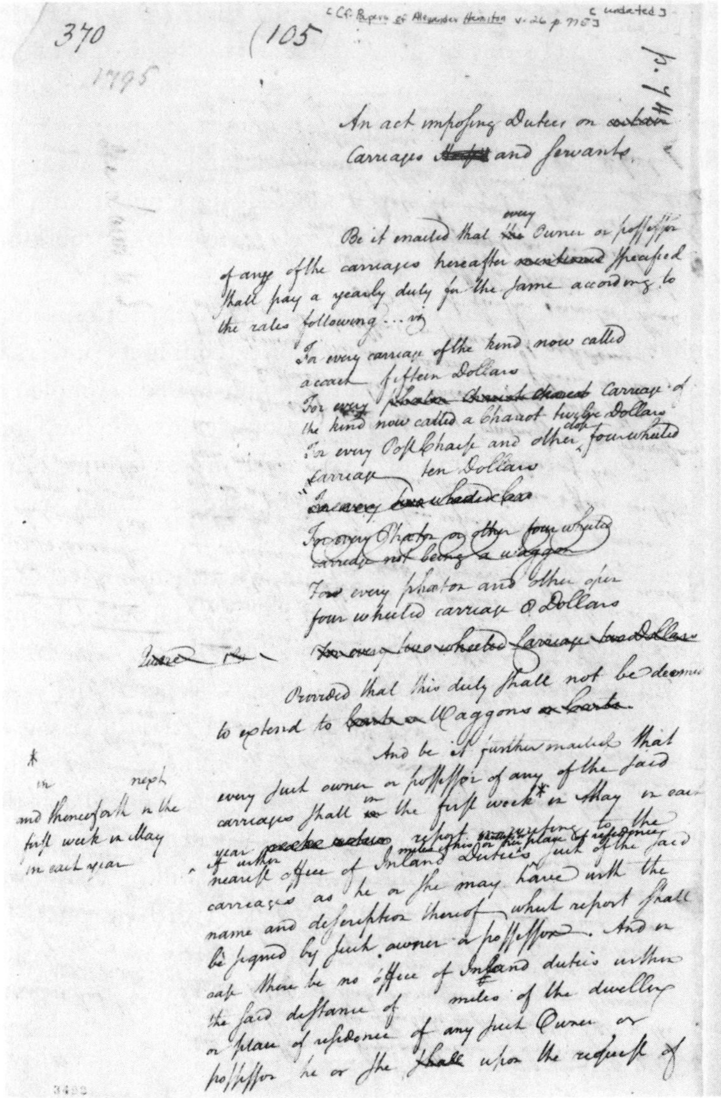
370 (105
[Cf. Papers of Alexander Hamilton v. 26 p. 77] [undated]
1795

An act imposing Duties on Carriages and Servants.

Be it enacted that every Owner or possessor of any of the carriages hereafter specified shall pay a yearly duty for the same according to the rates following...viz

For every carriage of the kind now called a coach fifteen Dollars

For every Carriage of the kind now called a Chariot twelve Dollars

For every Post Chaise and other four wheeled carriage ten Dollars

For every phaeton and other open four wheeled carriage 8 Dollars

Provided that this duty shall not be deemed to extend to Waggons

And be it further enacted that every such owner or possessor of any of the said carriages shall in the first week* in May in each year report to the nearest office of Inland Duties such of the said carriages as he or she may have with the name and description thereof which report shall be signed by such owner or possessor. And in case there be no office of Inland duties within the said distance of miles of the dwelling or place of residence of any such Owner or possessor he or she upon the request of

* and thenceforth in the first week in May in each year

Although Hamilton worked tirelessly to prepare his 1791 *Report on Manufactures,* as this page of the manuscript indicates, Congress did not accept his report and its proposals were not fulfilled until the nineteenth century, well after Hamilton's death in 1804. *Library of Congress, Manuscript Division, Alexander Hamilton Papers, Speeches and Writings File, 1778–1804*

Hamilton's third great report, his *Report on the Subject of Manufactures* (submitted to Congress on December 1, 1791), did not succeed, however.[5] This report, the apex of Hamilton's fiscal program, was his plan for launching the United States on an economic course moving to an economy with increasing commitment to commerce and particularly to manufacturing. Hamilton urged that the United States expand its economic base to include manufacturing and spelled out his reasoning for the change. Not only was manufacturing as productive as agriculture, he argued; it would benefit the farmers of America. Rejecting the idea that, if left to itself, the economy would generate the best results for society, Hamilton concluded that the government should influence economic actors for society's benefit.

The United States, he believed, should launch an ambitious program of encouraging local manufacturers. Hamilton proposed enacting tariffs to protect fledgling industries until they became securely established; awarding prizes for new developments in technology; controlling or prohibiting exports of raw materials; subsidizing key industries or projects; building a system of roads and canals to encourage domestic economic activity; adopting a system for regulating the quality of manufactured products; and encouraging inventions by paying bounties. Despite what later generations of economists and historians have hailed as his daring creativity in proposing innovative policy, Hamilton's report failed to win the support of Congress, and his ideas had to await fulfillment until the nineteenth century.

For Hamilton, understanding public administration was a vital complement to his vision of political economy. Public administration was a means for him to teach himself, and to teach those who were working under his leadership in the Treasury department, how to make that department work. Public administration endlessly fascinated Hamilton. He saw public administration as the body of ideas and principles by which he hoped to make government do its job, using its methods to vindicate his political and economic views.

Hamilton considered public administration as a set of supple and versatile tools to encourage economic prosperity and development as well as to sustain the federal government's fiscal health. Hamilton was the first great theorist of public administration in American history. Even at those times when most Americans have turned to worship at the ideological shrine of Thomas Jefferson, students of public administration have devoted close, admiring attention to Hamilton's thought and work. His economic thought and his thought on public administration reinforced and shaped each other.

Hamilton used ideas about public administration to define how he believed the federal government should give structure and purpose to the day-to-day running of government, in response to the ever-changing demands of public policy, economic life, and political advocacy. Although he never wrote a systematic treatise on the subject (though he often mentioned his desire to do so), he identified five principles at the core of his administrative vision. He crystallized these principles in five words—energy, unity, duration, power, and responsibility. These principles focused Hamilton's thinking and guided his running of the Treasury department and its oversight of the nation's economic life.

By the term "public administration," Hamilton meant the day-to-day approach to governing, going beyond the definition and advocacy of public policy to addressing the ordinary tasks of defining and running a government's processing of its business. In other words, the focus of public administration was the operation of the government's systems of regulation and taxation and of ensuring a smooth overseeing of government's daily transactions regarding ordinary people and enterprises. Hamilton believed that administration had been sensibly committed to the government's executive branch. Assigning administration to the legislative branch would work against public administration's needs for efficiency, coherence, and responsibility, leaving it prey to the interplay of competing interests that would block Congress from forming and putting into effect an effective national policy.

Within the general idea of public administration, Hamilton gave pride of place to energy. To Hamilton, energy meant vigor or strength in the government, focused in the executive branch—specifically in the Treasury department. The Constitution and federal statutes concentrated both the responsibility for running the government and the ability to carry out its policies in the Treasury, the executive branch's most important and powerful department.

In Hamilton's view, energy gave rise to four further important factors, all necessary to an effective system of public administration: unity, duration, adequacy, and responsibility:

- *Unity* of authority defined a vertical model of direction and command, from the Treasury Secretary down, promoting coherence in the definition and application of government policy and the clarification of its enforcement. Unity would make it possible for officials charged with the duties of administration and merchants who sought to meet administration's demands to share a clear understanding of what public policy would require and a commitment to achieving it.
- *Duration* had to do with the length of time during which the Secretary and his subordinates would hold authority consistent with forming a sense of responsibility for the proper exercise of energy in framing and carrying out the department's policies. It did no good to create an administrative system that had the energy to establish administrative policies if that system lacked the duration in office to give effect to those policies and to carry them out. So, too, the administrative process had to define a period for its action that was at once long enough in duration to permit the well-considered and systematic operation of the administrative process while also short enough to permit the efficient carrying-out of its administrative responsibilities for private parties and for the government.

- Hamilton also prized *an adequate grant of government power* that would enable the Treasury department and its officials to administer national policy. Having watched the Confederation's want of power too closely and for too long in the 1780s, Hamilton refused to tolerate a similar situation under the Constitution. Fortunately, the First Federal Congress shared his point of view and it crafted the Treasury department to correspond to that perspective; indeed, it benefited from Hamilton's behind-the-scenes assistance in framing the legislation setting up the Treasury department. So, too, in confirming President Washington's appointment of Hamilton as Treasury Secretary, the Senate also supported the Hamiltonian vision. Once he was in office, Congress sustained him by supporting most of his legislative proposals (though not those set forth in his 1791 *Report on Manufactures*).
- Finally, *responsibility* was vital to any system of public administration, and a valuable counterpart to the other elements of Hamilton's vision of effective public administration. From the Secretary down the line, all Treasury officials were responsible to the department and to the nation for how they administered public policy. Hamilton so valued responsibility that, in *The Federalist*, he defined and expounded three types of responsibility in government—legislative, executive, and judicial—and he explained how the Constitution would make all three versions of government responsibility feasible and enforceable in the constitutional system. So, too, Hamilton ran the Treasury department to ensure that Treasury officials would conduct themselves in a manner consistent with public administration's demands, in particular with the concept of executive responsibility.

Hamilton's synthesis of political economy and public administration undergirded his greatest efforts as the first secretary of the Treasury. From 1789 to 1795, Hamilton devoted himself to his creative blend of political economy, constitutional law, and public administration. His *Reports* set forth his ideas on economic policy-making, and his profound commitment to public administration gave institutional structure and energy to the Treasury department, and through it to the national economy. The extent of his achievement is captured by the later comment by Thomas Jefferson, blending envy and frustration: "We can pay off his debt in 15 years, but we can never get rid of his financial system."[6]

Chapter 5

War and Peace

In the late eighteenth century, issues of war and peace, and their consequences for nations and political systems old and new, often dominated events or lurked just below their surface. Whether in monarchies, empires, or republics, war and peace overshadowed the tempestuous decades of the Age of Enlightenment and the Age of the Democratic Revolution. Alexander Hamilton was one of that period's leading politicians; even when he was not embroiled in foreign affairs, matters of war and peace elbowed their way into his mind.

Hamilton sought to understand his world and the place of the United States in it. He saw his nation as large, rickety, and new, existing uneasily in an international order dominated by actual and potential conflict among great powers. Hamilton paid close attention as these powers competed for political, military, and economic dominance. All too often, as he knew, that competition burst the bounds of peacetime rivalry to plunge these nations into war. Such wars posed questions of survival for young, fragile nations such as the United States—questions that he deemed of paramount importance to the nation and its future.

Two events in Hamilton's experience had special urgency for the question of how the United States might preserve itself in peace in a hostile world. The first was the American Revolution, when the United States was fighting literally for its life in its War for Independence against Great Britain. The new nation had to defeat its former mother country's effort to regain control over the rebellious Americans. Then, nearly fifteen years later, the French Revolution ignited a series of wars that brought profound disruption to Europe and to the United States. In that era, the United States was an innocent bystander in a series of world diplomatic and military conflicts into which it tried to avoid being pulled. Both crises raised issues of definition for the American nation and its government, and for those, like Hamilton, who sought to define what that nation was, what it stood for, and what it would become.

In the late 1770s and early 1780s, Hamilton served his country as an American soldier. His rise in military rank was rapid—first as captain of a New York artillery company, then as a lieutenant colonel in the Continental Army and a trusted aide to General George Washington, and finally as the holder of a field command in the 1781 Battle of Yorktown. All the while, Hamilton also was an assiduous and precocious student of constitutional government and world affairs. Even after the end of the American War for Independence, Hamilton persisted in his efforts to give the United States the kind of government that would enable it to survive in a world dominated by conflict among great powers. In pursuing those inquiries, he sought to define the new nation for himself, for his contemporaries, and for posterity. His military and diplomatic investigations and his political and constitutional studies bolstered each other and gave each other not just meaning but urgency.

In the 1790s, as a key figure in the new American government under the Constitution of 1787, Hamilton confronted a world that was severely different from that of the American Revolution. The issue facing the United States was how to preserve American independence and national interests. Two oceans might seem to protect the United States from European wars, but Hamilton and his colleagues in the federal government had to keep their nation from becoming embroiled in a ruinous trans-Atlantic war arising from the rivalry between its former ally, France, and its former mother country, Great Britain. Making that challenge more vexing for Hamilton was his disagreement with other Americans who adopted different answers to looming questions about America and its future.

As it struggled in the throes of its revolution, France transformed from a monarchy into a republic. France deposed its king, Louis XVI, and tried, convicted, and executed him. Responding to those cataclysmic events, an alliance of conservative monarchies led by Great Britain declared war on France, and in turn the revolutionary French Republic declared war on them. These events plunged Europe into a continental war.

That European war posed many problems for the United States, flowing in part from the Americans' 1778 alliance with France and in part from what many Americans saw as the intellectual and political resonances between the American Revolution and the French Revolution. Americans divided swiftly in response to the war sparked by the French Revolution; that domestic political division grew in bitterness and urgency. Some Americans wanted the United States to remain neutral. Others argued that their nation should take the side of Britain and its conservative monarchical allies to oppose the radical French nation. Still others favored the cause of worldwide democratic revolution, a cause that they saw as symbolized and championed by revolutionary France; they brushed aside any doubts about French radicalism.

Hamilton saw neutrality as the best option for the United States; informing his choice was his distaste for and skepticism about the cause of France and its revolution. Jefferson favored the opposite choice, as did James Madison. Domestic partisan divisions trace their earliest roots to differences over Hamilton's fiscal policies, but these factional clashes soon meshed with parallel divisions over foreign policy. Worse, the clashing passions growing out of these domestic and foreign divisions cross-pollinated and intensified each other.

Hamilton never had any direct experience of diplomacy. As an officer on Washington's staff during the War for Independence, he occasionally had had dealings with military officers from other nations—a few times with officers from Britain but more regularly with officers from France, most notably his friend the Marquis de Lafayette. As the aide to Washington most fluent in French, Hamilton also often assisted Washington in communicating with America's French allies. Further, as Hamilton served at Washington's side, his respect for the Virginian's skills of military and political leadership flourished. Consider, for example, his eloquent praise of Washington's leadership during the Battle of Monmouth in 1778:

> I never saw the general to so much advantage. His coolness and firmness were admirable. He instantly took measures for checking the enemy's advance, and giving time for the army, which was very near, to form and make a proper disposition. . . . America owes a great deal to General Washington for the day's work. . . . By his own good sense and fortitude he turned the fate of the day. . . . he directed the whole with the skill of a Master workman. He did not hug himself at a distance and leave an Arnold to win laurels for him, but by his own presence, he brought order out of confusion, animated his troops and led them to success.[1]

Such encounters as these tested Hamilton's military discipline and his evolving views of American diplomacy. Thus, when he considered the president as commander-in-chief of the nation's armed forces, he wrote supporting that feature of the presidency with conviction grounded on experience:

> Of all the cares or concerns of government, the direction of war most peculiarly demands those qualities which distinguish the

> exercise of power by a single hand. The direction of war implies the direction of the common strength, and the power of directing and employing the common strength, focus an usual and essential part in the definition of the executive authority.[2]

After Hamilton became the nation's first secretary of the Treasury, he experienced the temptations and vexations of American foreign policy. In early 1790, for example, Hamilton engaged in informal talks with the British diplomat Major George Beckwith, aide-de-camp to the governor-general of Canada. Beckwith had come to New York City, then the new nation's capital, to persuade the US government to allow British military forces to cross American territory to attack Spain's Louisiana Territory. Hamilton assured Beckwith that President Washington would raise no objection to such a move by Britain. Insistent that he was expressing his own opinion only and not seeking to bind his nation by his words, Hamilton nonetheless assured Beckwith that President Washington would not oppose what the British proposed to do. At the same time, he also warned Beckwith, and through him Britain, against the views of Secretary of State Thomas Jefferson, whom he described as an American patriot but one stirred by feelings of friendship for France and hostility toward Great Britain. The result of Hamilton's candor was that British diplomats concluded that they need not take Jefferson seriously as an American diplomat; rather, they would see him as a man inspired by party sentiment and Anglophobia, despite his official diplomatic position. This was hardly a helpful opinion for Hamilton to have shared with a British diplomat, even in informal conversation. Over the next few years, Hamilton increasingly found himself in conflict with Jefferson over matters of foreign affairs as well as over domestic policy.

In the neutrality crisis of 1793, Hamilton did a constructive job of diplomatic advocacy despite Jefferson's opposition. He was the leading supporter in the Washington administration of American neutrality in European affairs. Neutrality seemed an excellent choice for the United States, which was seeking to avoid becoming involved in the war raging between Great Britain (and its allies) and France. On the desirability of an American policy of neutrality, he agreed with most of Washington's cabinet—except for Jefferson; he also was in alignment with the president. The case for neutrality that Hamilton made in cabinet meetings shaped two aspects of the American response to the neutrality crisis. First, the United States would embrace neutrality, abandoning the French-American alliance that had been established by the 1778 treaty between the two nations. Hamilton won that dispute by maintaining that that treaty had been between the United States and King Louis XVI, in 1778 the incarnation of French sovereignty. With the abolition of the monarchy, including the downfall and death of Louis XVI and the establishment of the French Republic, Hamilton concluded, the 1778 treaty was at an end. Thus, there was no alliance between the United States and the French Republic. Second, as Hamilton insisted, President Washington could decide on his own to commit the United States to neutrality, invoking his power as president to decide this and other questions of the nation's foreign policy.

Though the neutrality issue seemed settled by Washington's proclamation, backed up by the cabinet's endorsement, the issue soon found its way into public debate. Hamilton, as was often the case, took the lead in bringing his views to the nation's newspapers. In a series of newspaper essays written as Pacificus justifying Washington's proclamation of neutrality, Hamilton made a powerful case for presidential authority in foreign relations under the Constitution:

> The President is the constitutional Executor of the laws. Our Treaties and the laws of Nations form a part of the laws of the land. He who is to execute the laws must first judge for himself of their meaning. In order to the observance of that conduct, which the laws of nations combined with our treaties prescribed to this country, in reference to the present War in Europe, it was neces-

> sary for the President to judge for himself whether there was any thing in our treaties incompatible with an adherence to neutrality. Having judged that there was not, he had a right, and if in his opinion the interests of the Nation required it, it was his duty as Executor of the laws, to proclaim the neutrality of the Nation, to exhort all persons to observe it, and to warn them of the penalties which would attend its non observance.[3]

Madison, at the behest of Jefferson, launched his own thoughtful, eloquent series of essays answering Hamilton as Helvidius. Not even Madison, however, could overcome the strength and persuasiveness of Hamilton's arguments for Washington's decision to keep the nation neutral. The debate between Pacificus and Helvidius has stood for more than two centuries as the greatest exposition of contrasting views on the Constitution's arrangements for foreign policy and diplomacy; in the 1790s Hamilton won that debate.

Modern experts on the Constitution and on American foreign policy have often identified Hamilton as a forerunner of the school of realism in international relations; realists often maintain that nations engage in coldly rational disagreements over their assertions of national interest, with no higher or more idealistic guide to national conduct. It is possible to read Hamilton that way, and yet Hamilton was equally preoccupied in linking arguments about foreign relations with matters of honor and credit abroad; he argued that honor and realism were not antithetical but complementary. He based his stand as Pacificus on this honor-grounded viewpoint on American diplomacy.

As secretary of state, Jefferson was the nation's chief diplomat and President Washington's designated advisor on foreign policy. He was the cabinet member with the clear institutional and personal mandate in that sphere. And yet Hamilton sometimes meddled in that field, as in his informal 1790 discussions with Beckwith and in his Pacificus essays three years later. At such times, what drove Hamilton was his certitude that his was the right approach and that Jefferson's was the wrong approach, no matter what political or institutional barriers stood before them. If need be, Hamilton thought, he could frame and publish authoritative arguments for his views on foreign policy addressed to what later generations would call the court of public opinion. President Washington retained final authority to establish the nation's role in world affairs, and he recognized Jefferson's senior role on that subject in his administration—and yet he also paid heed to Hamilton's views. In part, Washington did so because he recognized that issues of economics, trade, and commerce (on which Hamilton had significant claims to speak and argue with authority) had foreign as well as domestic significance; he also listened to Hamilton out of abiding respect for Hamilton as a senior advisor who often shared the president's viewpoint.

Hamilton also devoted extensive consideration to developing his understanding of war—its uses, its limits, and the ways in which it was fought. War was a central part of Hamilton's intellectual world. His service as a soldier exposed him to the complex and multifaceted issues of war at a critical period of his life, as well as at a crucial time in the life of the American nation. Hamilton's experiences in war and politics cemented his role as a leading national advisor on questions of war and of peace. His first adult political role was as an artillery officer in 1775; Washington then came to know and trust him both as a soldier and a loyal aide. In the Confederation years and during the framing and adoption of the Constitution and the nation's first decade under the Constitution, Hamilton established himself as a civilian who thought deeply about issues of foreign and military affairs in helping to devise a fledgling constitutional republic. Even after he stepped down from Washington's administration in 1795, Hamilton returned to Washington's side in 1796 to assist his former chief in composing a final presidential address from Washington to his countrymen; the Farewell Address distilled Washington's (and Hamilton's) advice to posterity on the presidency and on constitutional government. Finally, from 1798 to

1800, during the "quasi-war" crisis with France, Hamilton served as the second in command of the army mustered by the Adams administration under Washington's command to counteract threats of war from France.

Those last two roles juxtaposed one of Hamilton's most successful engagements (politically and substantively) with issues of war and peace with his least successful effort in that sphere. The work that Hamilton did with Washington in 1796 highlighted his remarkable skill as ghostwriter and collaborator with the first president in spelling out wise counsel for future presidents and for future citizens. By contrast, Hamilton's uncharacteristically inept involvement with the Adams administration exemplified the corrosive effects that partisan disagreements had on American public life, domestic and foreign, during John Adams's presidency.

The hostility between Adams and Hamilton had taken shape beginning in 1789, when Adams had become vice president and Hamilton was about to be named Treasury Secretary. Adams disdained Hamilton's youth and what he saw as the younger man's lack of political and diplomatic experience; for his part, Hamilton returned Adams's dislike, focusing on what he disdained as Adams's pomposity and prolixity.

The bad relationship between Adams and Hamilton got worse when Adams succeeded Washington as president in 1797 but kept Washington's cabinet as his own—even though his cabinet members felt no loyalty to him. Secretary of State Timothy Pickering, Secretary of the Treasury Oliver Wolcott, and Secretary of War James McHenry were loyal instead to Washington, their former chief, or to Hamilton, their political leader. Indeed, they regularly sought advice from Hamilton, eager to conceal from Adams their repeated consultations with a private lawyer in New York City. Hamilton ignored any qualms that he might have felt about interfering with the administration of President Adams, whom he dismissed as an absentee president. Rather,

Hamilton treated Adams's apparent unwillingness to lead his administration as a virtual authorization to Hamilton to lead the government for him. Indeed, Hamilton interfered so much in Adams's administration because he treated the loyalty of Adams's cabinet secretaries to him as informal permission to lead that government, in particular on issues of war and peace. The result was the risk of further military adventures, most notably the "quasi-war."

When the quasi-war began, Adams asked ex-president Washington to command American forces; Washington then sought to name Hamilton as major general and the army's inspector general despite Adams's opposition. When Adams reluctantly conceded the point, Hamilton seemed ready to lead the army into a real war with France despite Adams's doubts. Fortunately for the nation, in 1800, following Washington's death in December 1799, Adams once again took charge of his administration. He had towering brawls with his cabinet, all of whom he forced to resign or fired, and with Hamilton; Adams then installed new cabinet members who worked with him to end the quasi-war, to disband the army, and to stave off any future hostilities between France and the United States. Hamilton's part in these events shows him falling prey over and over again to lapses in judgment and spasms of egotism, shortsightedness, and bad temper.

In retrospect, despite his erratic, undisciplined, and overwrought disagreements with President Adams, Hamilton stands in posterity's memory as the leading advocate among the founding fathers of executive authority in foreign affairs and in matters of war and peace. Most notably in his Pacificus essays, he made an authoritative and eloquent case for the president's independence as the nation's chief diplomat, in particular for his ability to proclaim American neutrality based solely on his constitutional authority as president. Hamilton also spoke persuasively for presidential command over the nation's military and naval power. And, in his collaboration with George Washington in framing Washington's

Farewell Address, Hamilton aided Washington's efforts to define the lasting legacies of his presidency for future generations. These achievements do much to outweigh Hamilton's failures of judgment in the late 1790s, in particular his quixotic and ill-advised efforts to take charge of John Adams's administration and its thorny, tangled relations with France.

Chapter 6

Honor and Dueling

While seeking to transcend his era, Alexander Hamilton still was firmly rooted in it; he shared this trait with the other first-rank founding fathers, including Thomas Jefferson. The hooks that linked Jefferson to his time were slavery and the ideas and assumptions growing out of it; the hook that linked Hamilton to his time was honor culture. Honor was a central theme of Hamilton's life and political thought, as it was for many of his contemporaries. Honor culture was the framework within which Hamilton situated himself and his ideas; honor shaped and pervaded his understandings of politics, constitutionalism, political economy, public administration, war, and peace. Honor culture was a vital component of politics for all politicians during the eras of the American Revolution and the new republic.

Dueling was to honor as a fence was to a farm. Dueling defined and policed the limits of honor culture; it was the means by which honor fixed the metes and bounds of appropriate conduct for gentlemen. Gentlemen were elevated by birth and social standing above the common or middling sort; the political assumptions of Hamilton's time reserved roles of political leadership for gentlemen.

The first and only home owned by Alexander Hamilton (1802–1804) was the Grange, which he named after his family's ancestral home in Scotland; it stands in the Hamilton Heights neighborhood in Upper Manhattan. The house was home to his 1,000-volume library. Now a National Park Service historic site, the Grange was moved from its original location to the campus of City College of New York. *Edwin Davis French, engraver / Library of Congress, LC-DIG-pga-12806*

Custom sorted gentlemen into two categories—gentlemen of extreme politeness and gentlemen of the sword. Gentlemen of extreme politeness conducted themselves with profound discretion, saying no word and committing no deed that would risk embroiling them in an honor dispute. James Madison, for example, was a gentleman of extreme politeness. And yet gentlemen of extreme politeness could still advise friends about issues of honor. Though Madison himself never got entangled in an honor dispute, he made himself available as an advisor in such disputes to such friends as James Monroe, who sought Madison's counsel when, for example, he thought that he was risking ensnarement in an honor dispute with President John Adams.

As a gentleman of the sword, Monroe was freer with his words than Madison was, even hot-tempered. The difference between Madison and Monroe was that, as a gentleman of the sword, Monroe could be less restrained with his words, provided that he was prepared to answer for his words if they embroiled him in an honor dispute. One central trait of gentlemen of the sword was that they had seen military service; for example, Monroe, Hamilton, and Burr, all gentlemen of the sword, all had been officers in the Continental Army during the American Revolution. Though the army's rules forbade duels and honor disputes, honor disputes still happened, sometimes spilling out of control to become duels.

Modern lawyers would recognize that an honor dispute was a type of alternative dispute resolution. Like alternative dispute resolution, honor disputes took place outside the formal legal system. Also like alternative dispute resolution, honor disputes had their own formalities and rules, rooted in the code of honor, parallel to both the opening and the working out of legal disputes. Nonetheless, as a use of potentially lethal violence to resolve a conflict over honor, dueling was in direct conflict with the rule of law. This clash between the law and the code of honor was to haunt Hamilton, who was both a lawyer and a gentleman of the sword.

At stake in a dispute over honor was the reputation of both parties—that of the complainant, who believed that his honor had been injured by the insult that he had suffered, and that of the respondent, who had to stand up for or to explain away or even to apologize for his allegedly insulting words. An honor dispute began when the complainant spoke or wrote to the respondent, referencing certain words written or spoken in public by the respondent about the complainant that seemed to injure his honor; the complainant then demanded that the respondent apologize for or explain or defend those words. The parties to the dispute had to be of equal social status; otherwise, the controversy could not go forward. For example, if a journalist (by definition not a gentleman) insulted a gentleman, the result would be neither a negotiation nor a duel. Rather, the insulted gentleman might seize a cane and beat the offending journalist in the street.

Sometimes, in response to a demand for explanation or justification, the respondent would give an innocent explanation for the words at issue; if so, the complainant could declare himself satisfied, ending the matter. The same result followed an offer of explanation and apology. Sometimes, however, the dispute could not be resolved so easily. In such cases, when the respondent answered the complainant by defending his words, an intricate dance of negotiation would follow. In that negotiation, both the complainant and the respondent, the principals in the honor dispute, would ask trusted friends to act for them as seconds. The seconds would speak to each other and would consult with their respective principals, who would not speak to each other directly but would speak only with their own seconds. If the seconds could work out a settlement or compromise between the principals, the dispute would be resolved and the principals and the seconds would issue a joint statement reporting that settlement.

Only if a compromise could not be reached would arrangements for a duel begin. Those arrangements, negotiated by the seconds, would cover such matters as the choice of weapons and of the location where the duel would be fought, the setting of the date and time when the duel would be fought, the choice of a physician, and the defining of whatever other rules might seem appropriate. Even after an honor dispute became a duel, there was still a chance that last-minute negotiations could avert it.

If the parties could not resolve the dispute peaceably, the principals, the seconds, and the physician would go to the agreed-upon dueling ground at the chosen date and time, bringing the weapons agreed on to be used in the duel. (In most American duels, the weapons chosen would be pistols.) The seconds would oversee the duel's conduct. They would pace off the distance between the principals, would supervise the loading of the pistols, and then would hand a pistol to each principal. The duelists would take their positions, face each other, and raise their pistols. One second would count time off, as agreed under the rules negotiated. At the second's call, "Present!," the duelists would fire at each other. Each duelist was to fire in the direction of his opponent; aiming was not really possible, as dueling pistols were not notably accurate. The duel's object was that the duelists would risk killing and risk being killed, rather than setting out to kill. After the first shot, if both parties were still standing, the seconds would ask, "Is honor satisfied?" If both parties said, "Yes," then the duel was over, and the principals and the seconds would quit the field. If either or both said "No," the duel would resume, and the seconds would assist the principals in preparing for another round of fire. The duel would continue, round by round, until one party fell to the other's fire or until both parties confirmed that honor had been satisfied, ending the duel.

Though the disputes that gave rise to most duels were matters of personal honor, some duels were also political duels, occasioned by a dispute rooted in political factionalism. Such duels usually arose immediately following an election. In those cases, either the leader of a losing party or one of his supporters would challenge the leader of the winning party or another distinguished figure in that party. No matter what the ostensible cause, the duel's purpose was for both duelists to vindicate their honor (or their party's honor, for which they stood surety, a legal term denoting how each duelist would assume responsibility for defending his party as well as himself).

Duels—particularly political duels—were also about public opinion. The public was the audience before whom the duel was fought, even though the public was not actually present to witness the duel. The public's opinion of the duelists' honor, as tested by the duel, was what mattered; the public would judge the duel based on its conduct and on its outcome, as reported by the duelists and the seconds. This appeal to public opinion again put dueling in open conflict with, and thus in violation of, the rule of law.

Hamilton took part, as principal or as second, in more than a dozen different affairs of honor, from his time as an officer of the Continental Army during the Revolution through the turbulent 1790s until his final, fatal honor dispute in 1804 with Aaron Burr. None of the previous honor disputes had resulted in a duel; rather, all had been negotiated to a peaceful resolution. The number of these disputes, however, suggests Hamilton's propensity for contention and his sensitivity about his honor. Hamilton's honor disputes during the Revolution occurred along fault lines dividing various conflicting groups of generals and inferior officers in the Continental Army. Those arising between 1790 and 1804 pitted Hamilton against various Republican politicians. Burr had faced three previous honor disputes, two with Hamilton (both resolved without a duel) and the third with Hamilton's brother-in-law John Barker Church (resulting in a duel that caused no injury to either party). Thus, both Hamilton and Burr had had ample experience with the code of honor.

Burr and Hamilton had known each other for decades and had much in common. Both had been college-educated Continental Army officers during the Revolution. Burr had spent two stormy weeks in 1776 as an aide to George Washington until he left Washington's staff, to both men's relief; Hamilton joined Washington's staff early in 1777 and lasted four years as Washington's principal aide. Burr and Hamilton were both leading members of the New York bar, sometimes serving as co-counsel in major cases and sometimes appearing opposite each other. Both men were active in New York and national politics. Although Burr took no public position on whether to ratify the US Constitution, whereas Hamilton led the Constitution's supporters, they ended up on opposite sides of the divide between Federalists and Republicans. For example, in 1791 Burr had defeated General Philip Schuyler, Hamilton's father-in-law, in Schuyler's attempt to win re-election to the US Senate from New York. Burr and Hamilton were known to be political rivals, though they were apparently personally friendly. They even resembled each other: both were short, slight of build, with the impeccable bearing characteristic of veteran soldiers.

Though political mythology roots the Burr-Hamilton duel in the presidential election of 1800, chronology argues against that explanation, as four years separated that election and the duel. The true proximate cause of their honor dispute was the New York gubernatorial contest of 1804. The Republicans had nominated Morgan Lewis. Dissident Republicans who called themselves Burrites had rallied behind the vice president. Burr was not just the Burrite candidate for governor in 1804, however. In 1800 and 1801, Federalists had considered backing Burr against Jefferson in the Jefferson-Burr tie for president in the Electoral College; in 1802, Burr had made overtures to New York's Federalists, and Federalists remembered Burr's efforts. Now, in 1804, the Federalists threw their political weight behind Burr as their gubernatorial candidate. Horrified, Hamilton plunged into a whirlwind of political activity backing Lewis and opposing Burr. Lewis won the election. Humiliated by his loss, Burr swore to challenge the first man of note on the other side who presented himself. That man turned out to be Hamilton.

Burr came across a letter reprinted in a newspaper, the *Albany Argus,* from Rev. Charles Cooper to General Philip Schuyler, both Federalists. In his letter, Cooper noted Hamilton's words and conduct in campaigning against Burr. After quoting some of Hamilton's language condemning Burr, Cooper wrote, "I could detail to you a still more despicable opinion which General Hamilton has expressed of Mister Burr." Burr focused on the phrase "despicable opinion" and wrote to Hamilton to demand an explanation. Burr's demand set off a two-week series of letters, first between Burr and Hamilton and then between the two men's seconds, William P. Van Ness for Burr and Nathaniel Pendleton for Hamilton.

Answering Burr's demand, Hamilton protested that he had said many derogatory things about Burr; thus, he did not know what opinion was the focus of Burr's demand. He then engaged in a protracted quibble about the meaning of the word "despicable," an exercise in logic-chopping that only angered Burr further.[1] The dispute went back and forth, achieving nothing except exasperating both Burr and Hamilton, until an angered Burr raised the stakes very high. He insisted that Hamilton tender an apology for all the critical things that he had ever said about Burr for the previous fifteen years (since 1789) and also that Hamilton promise that he would never say anything derogatory about Burr again. Hamilton retorted that no man could with honor give such an undertaking. Burr then issued a formal challenge to Hamilton, which Hamilton accepted. At this point, the negotiations between Burr and Hamilton shifted from avoiding a duel to deciding when, where, and how a duel between them would take place.

There are a few salient points about how this honor dispute escalated—or deteriorated—into a duel. First, what if Burr had gone first to Cooper to ask what Hamilton's "despicable opinion" had been and then confronted Hamilton with his exact words (if Cooper had provided them)? Those words have long been what the director Alfred Hitchcock would have called the duel's MacGuffin (a device that, without intrinsic importance, triggers the plot of a movie)—but the existence of an unspecified "despicable opinion," rather than what the opinion actually was, had led to the duel. Had Burr learned what he wanted to know from Cooper, that fact might have shortened the correspondence between Burr and Hamilton but still produced the same result—a duel. Or, had Cooper refused to reveal Hamilton's words, Burr would have been trapped without recourse. Second, Burr's choice to confront Hamilton rather than Cooper suggests how ready he was to accept a duel as the only way to resolve his dispute with Hamilton and vindicate his honor. Third, had Burr been that ready to risk a duel, Hamilton could not have avoided it.

One more thing may have relevance to this duel—Hamilton's informal role in a previous duel, in 1801. His oldest son Philip had gotten into an altercation with a young Burrite, George Eacker, who insisted on raising their honor dispute to the level of a duel. Troubled, Philip consulted his father, who did his best to advise Philip about the code of honor. Hamilton did not realize how perilous Philip's situation was, however. In their duel, Eacker mortally wounded Philip; when Dr. David Hosack, a family friend and the physician present at the duel, told Hamilton of the duel's result and his son's grave condition, the distraught Hamilton fainted. Hamilton fainted again at Philip's funeral. Guilt tortured him for years thereafter, and may have shaped his response to his own honor dispute with Burr.

Burr and Hamilton had locked themselves into fighting a duel. They would meet on the field of honor—on the dueling ground at Weehawken, New Jersey, across the Hudson River from New York City's Greenwich Village, on July 11, 1804. (It was the same place where George Eacker had mortally wounded Philip Hamilton.) In the days before the "interview at Weehawken," Hamilton and Burr prepared their wills and made other final arrangements. In particular, Hamilton wrote two letters to his wife, insisting that she would understand why he had to risk his life in a duel—to preserve his ability to be "in future useful." In other words, Hamilton had to defend his honor to be eligible to be once again a political leader. Burr also was willing to fight a duel to preserve his honor at the risk of his life, that essential qualification to be a political leader once again. Unlike Burr, however, Hamilton felt an obligation to ponder the conflict facing him within the context formed by three different sets of rules—the code of honor; the laws of New York and of New Jersey, which prohibited dueling; and the principles of Christianity, which dueling also violated. In light of his realization of these facts, Hamilton decided not to fire directly at Burr, confiding his decision to no one.

These facts were the foundation of which the fatal encounter between Burr and Hamilton took place at the dueling ground in Weehawken, New Jersey, at sunrise on July 11, 1804. The duelists, accompanied by their seconds, William P. Van Ness and Nathaniel

Pendleton, and by Dr. David Hosack, arrived at the dueling ground and began their preparations. As the seconds measured the ground and established where Burr and Hamilton would stand, the two boatmen stood with their backs to the dueling ground so that they could swear truthfully later that they had not seen any part of the duel.

Burr and Hamilton took their places on the dueling ground and both men accepted the pistols that their seconds had loaded and handed to them. They were the same pistols that Burr had used in his duel with John Barker Church. The pistols had hair-triggers, but when asked if they should be set, Hamilton answered, "Not this time." He then put on his spectacles and squinted into the sun. Once the duelists were in position, the seconds took their positions to supervise the conduct of the duel.

When the count reached the appropriate time and the call of "Present!" came, the shots rang out at almost the same time. Burr's bullet struck Hamilton, passed through his liver, and lodged in his spine. When Hamilton fired, his bullet soared into the air above Burr and clipped a tree branch three feet above his head. Hamilton may not have been aware that he had fired; his gun may have gone off when Burr's bullet hit him.

When Hamilton was hit, he rose on his toes, spun, and collapsed with his face in the dirt. Dr. Hosack and Pendleton ran to Hamilton's side, knelt by the wounded man, and raised him from the ground; Hamilton gasped, "This is a mortal wound, Doctor," and fainted. Dr. Hosack, Pendleton, and their boatman carried Hamilton down to their rowboat and started the melancholy trip back across the river to Greenwich Village. At one point, Hamilton briefly revived, saw his pistol lying in the bottom of the rowboat, and said, "Take care of that pistol—it is cocked. It may go off and do mischief."[2] Then he fainted again. Hamilton did not realize that he had already fired his pistol.

When Burr saw Hamilton fall, he threw his pistol aside and ran toward the fallen man. Van Ness grasped his arm and pulled him away, opening an umbrella to conceal Burr from view. They returned with their boatman to their rowboat and headed back across the river. All the way to New York, Burr kept saying, "I must go and speak to him."[3] Later that day, he sent an urgent inquiry to Dr. Hosack about Hamilton's condition.

On reaching Manhattan, Dr. Hosack and Pendleton carried the unconscious Hamilton from the river's edge to the house of Hamilton's friend William Bayard on Jane Street. There they tried to make Hamilton as comfortable as possible. But Hamilton had been grievously wounded. In an era when the only way to treat pain was by administering pain relief orally, Dr. Hosack could give him no relief at all; he could not even give Hamilton a drink of water. Friends summoned Hamilton's wife; at first, they feared to reveal the true cause of her husband's condition and told her only that he was experiencing "spasms." Though suffering intense pain, he was able to speak with those gathered around his bed. In particular, he spoke with the Episcopal bishop of New York City, who gave him holy communion. Hamilton lingered into the afternoon of the next day. He died on July 12 at 2 P.M., with his wife and seven surviving children gathered around him.

After the duel, Burr fled New York City and headed south. Ultimately, he reached the region along the Mississippi River, where most whom Burr encountered applauded his conduct in the duel as honorable. Burr stood trial for treason (on a matter not connected with his duel with Hamilton) in federal court in Virginia in 1807, but the jury declined to convict him or to acquit him, rendering a verdict of "not proven." Burr then fled to Europe, not returning to New York until 1810. For the rest of his life, he practiced law quietly in New York City, accepting the infamy resulting from the duel with mocking self-satire. He died in 1836, at the age of eighty.

Hamilton's funeral was one of the greatest public events that New York City had ever seen. His old friend and political ally, Gouverneur Morris, who had served with him at the Federal Convention in 1787, delivered the eulogy. Hamilton was buried in the graveyard of Trinity Church, near the corner of Broadway and Rector Street; when his wife died in 1854, half a century later, she was buried near him. Alexander Hamilton now rests in the heart of the nation's financial district, a monument to his efforts to fulfill his lifelong vision of a wealthy, powerful, and independent United States.

Epilogue

The Legacies of Alexander Hamilton

Understanding Alexander Hamilton's legacies requires us to consider not just the history that Hamilton made but also Hamilton in the light of that history. Hamilton's posthumous reputation falls into four stages. At first, these stages parallel those that historians have identified in Jefferson's historical reputation. When Jefferson's reputation has risen, Hamilton's has fallen, and vice versa, as if the two statesmen have been riding opposite ends of a seesaw. The recent phases of the story, however, have been more complicated.

The first stage, spanning the period from Hamilton's death to the outbreak of the Civil War in 1861, displays a blurred and diffuse Hamilton. Differing views of him clashed, failing to coalesce. The founding era was—and still is—a major source of American political mythology; that time's conflicts have continued to shape the American experiment's meaning. This fusion of history and legend began with Hamilton's death and extended through the first several decades of the nineteenth century. For those who insisted on refighting the political battles of Hamilton's life, or who treated the conflicts of their own time as recapitulating earlier clashes and reverberating after the duel, Hamilton remained as controversial in death as in life. The Jeffersonian vision of America as an agrarian utopia had prevailed, all but blotting out the Hamiltonian vision of the nation as a potentially great political, military, and economic power. The Jacksonian vision followed, congruent with Jeffersonianism in most respects and equally antithetical to the Hamiltonian worldview. As a result, few Americans venerated Hamilton beyond his family and his dwindling cohort of political allies. He existed as a perennial adversary but not as a model statesman.

Two of his sons, James Alexander Hamilton and John Church Hamilton, were their father's leading advocates, spurred by devotion to their father's memory, loyalty to their mother (who encouraged them until her death in 1854), and commitment to Hamilton's ideas and achievements. They sought to preserve Hamilton's historical reputation and to combat his vilification by Jeffersonians. James Hamilton recalled his father in his memoirs; John Church Hamilton published volume after volume of biography and history and an edition of his father's papers. Both sons hoped to fix a positive image of their father in posterity's memory.

Despite the Hamilton brothers' efforts, Alexander Hamilton seemed a figure of purely historical interest to most Americans in the decades following his death. They remembered him not for his ideas or for his achievements but rather for his role in the party battles of the 1790s and for his legendary duel with the equally legendary Aaron Burr. Hamilton's ideas were fading as much as he was. Hamilton's early death cost him the chance to order his legacy for posterity; further, there were few lawyers trained by Hamilton who were promoting his nationalist versions of constitutionalism and law. The constellation of principles linked to Jefferson, Andrew Jackson, and their partisans dominated the political, constitutional and intellectual world of the early nineteenth century.

In the 1860s, a constitutional, political, and military cataclysm shattered the Constitution as it was in 1861 and the structure of Jeffersonian and Jacksonian values undergirding it. Only then, in the second period of his posthumous history, did Hamilton sup-

Alexander Hamilton was buried at the graveyard of New York City's Trinity Church, at the corner of Wall Street and Broad Street. His widow, Elizabeth Schuyler Hamilton, was buried near him in 1854, half a century later. *Detroit Publishing Company photograph collection, Library of Congress, LC-DIG-det-4a22879*

plant Jefferson in stature. That period lasted more than seventy years, from the Civil War of 1861–1865 to the Great Depression of 1929–1941. The Union's victory in 1865 brought the abolition of slavery and destroyed the political might and cultural and economic authority of "the slave power" and its states'-rights constitutional vision; as a result, it also raised Hamilton to prominence in his countrymen's historical memory. Victorious Unionists gave Hamilton major intellectual credit for the Union's triumph, presenting him as the architect and advocate of American Union, national identity, material prosperity, and economic development. Some even named Hamilton progenitor of the late nineteenth century's rise of big business and of its ideological twin, laissez-faire capitalism. Political foes of Hamilton's apologists responded by casting Hamilton as the villain of the American political narrative.

In 1929, an economic cataclysm ignited a new political, intellectual, and cultural upheaval in American life and culture as seismic as that unleashed by the Civil War. Among the Great Depression's results was another reversal of polarity between Hamilton and Jefferson as cultural icons. The former hero of the booming economy became the villain of the stock market crash because posterity saw him as capitalism's champion; at the same time, Jefferson, his historic adversary, became the avatar of democracy. This third stage of Hamilton's posthumous reputation lasted from the 1930s until the 1970s—but its dichotomy was not so stark as that seen in the first two stages. Consider the oft-quoted synthesis of the New Deal: "Hamiltonian means to Jeffersonian ends." The phrase, often attributed to Franklin D. Roosevelt, was actually coined by the Progressive political theorist Herbert Croly, whose work Roosevelt knew and valued.

Both Hamilton and Jefferson were part of the Progressive movement's and the New Deal's intellectual heritage; the political and intellectual opposition that had once existed between them no longer explained their contrasting positions in historical and public memory. Twentieth-century constitutional theorists valued Hamilton's creative approach to federal governmental power, particularly his championing of a versatile and muscular executive. Students of public administration increasingly admired Hamilton as the subject's first great American theorist. As New Dealers devised administrative agencies to wrestle with the American economy's regulatory problems, they turned to Hamilton for intellectual authority and support.

Interest in Hamilton's thought in the twentieth century generated a steady trickle of biographies and monographs devoted to him. These books focused on Hamilton's constitutional, legal, administrative, and political thought and achievements—studying the public man in the public realm. Even so, Hamilton's students and admirers were comparatively few, outnumbered by the legions who revered Jefferson, whom President Roosevelt celebrated as the creator of America's democratic philosophy.

A fourth, more troubled era of the Founders' posthumous reputation did not begin until the 1960s. Jefferson was the initial victim of this new process of historical reconsideration. The blows to Jefferson's reputation had to do with his views of civil liberties and of slavery and race, including his record as a slaveowner, his "scientific" views of race, and the question of his relationship with his slave Sally Hemings.

At first, Jefferson stood alone as a target of efforts to wear down his historical reputation, but scholarly reconsideration soon spread to include the other founders, including Hamilton. What reasons spurred this reconsideration of Jefferson and his contemporaries? One was the publication of comprehensive scholarly editions of the papers of Jefferson, Hamilton, Adams, Washington, Madison, and other founding fathers; these editions helped to make intellectual reconsideration possible. The historian William W. Freehling rightly called this transformative form of scholarship "the documentary-editing revolution"; Freehling has suggested that these projects might have a greater effect on understanding American history than any one scholar's work. The documentary-editing projects, which make it possible for us to know these men better than they knew themselves, began in the 1940s; they combined historical veneration with scholarly reinterpretation. The rigorous, close-focus reconsideration made possible by these projects generated searching, skeptical revision rather than pious commemoration.

Side by side with the documentary-editing revolution came other changes in historical scholarship, spurred by the civil rights movement, the women's rights movement, and the campaign for the rights of Native Americans. New scholars, and older scholars asking new questions, challenged the prevailing historical narrative as unduly dominated by white men, political elites, and conventional models of politics. These scholars helped to transform the writing and teaching of history. Understanding the life and thought of a historical figure who owned slaves and lived off their labor changes—sometimes subtly, sometimes dramatically—when slaveholding becomes central to defining who that person was. The same is true for those who, while not owning slaves themselves, seemed indifferent to slavery's presence in the nation that they sought to create. A founding father's eloquent words about liberty take on ironic overtones when we recall that he owned slaves or accepted slavery as a fact of life lacking moral significance, even describing enslaved Africans as inferior to white people.

At first, Hamilton and Adams seemed destined for appreciative rediscovery. For Adams, a best-selling 2001 biography by the popular historian David McCullough made the difference; McCullough's book was followed by an HBO cable television miniseries based on it starring Paul Giamatti and Laura Linney. For Hamilton, the first transformative factor was Ron Chernow's celebratory biography, published in 2004. Next came Lin-Manuel Miranda's *Hamilton: An American Musical*, which took Broadway and the nation by storm in 2015. Reading Chernow's book inspired Miranda to create a hip-hop musical based on Hamilton's life. Casting nonwhite actors as white founding fathers, Miranda gave African American and Hispanic men and women a stake in the American founding narrative. The breathtaking success of *Hamilton* elevated "the ten-dollar Founding Father" in the public mind as a new American hero. Some historians objected to facets of the play—its presentation of Hamilton as a proto-abolitionist, its sketchy treatment of slavery, its elision of Hamilton's political conservatism and elitism. Others saw the play as an American example of "Shakespeare history" that reshaped history and omitted key historical facts for dramatic effect while seeking to remain true to history's human dimension.

In the wake of *Hamilton*, some historians have given Adams and Hamilton "the Jefferson treatment." For example, they have noted comments by Adams in his letters indicating his jaundiced views of African Americans, and his acceptance of slavery as a constant of human history (undermining his supposed status as a proto-abolitionist). More recently, while conceding that Hamilton helped to found the New-York Manumission Society and the state's first African free school, historians have pointed out Hamilton's largely passive view of slavery, noting that he sold slaves at the request of his father-in-law, the general and New York politician (and slaveowner) Philip Schuyler. Also, scholars have noted the omission of Native Americans from Miranda's play and have cited Hamilton's call in *The Federalist* No. 24 for strengthening federal military forces for such purposes as countering "the savage tribes on our Western frontier [who] ought to be regarded as our natural enemies."[1] (This quotation aligned Hamilton with most American politicians of his era, distinguished and obscure.)

In our time, many people have demanded reinterpretation of the nation's past, challenging whom we venerate with statues, monuments, memorials, and commemoration in the names of august institutions. In response, we have taken down statues, renamed buildings and streets, and removed such symbols as the Confederate battle flag, prompting heated denunciations in return. Disputes about the historical past seem fated to continue without end.

What, then, are we to make of Alexander Hamilton? His admittedly imperfect life should not leach away the value of his thought, nor should it erase what we can learn from him. Instead, we should focus on what Hamilton may still have to teach us about the bodies of ideas to which he contributed so much—constitutional government and law, economics and public administration, foreign policy, and the honest practice of politics with attention to standards of honor. Throughout the more than two centuries since his death, we have sought guidance from Hamilton at times of constitutional and economic crisis. Those times are when we need him most—and when he comes to the fore.

NOTES

Chapter 1

1. AH to Edward Stevens, November 11, 1769, in Joanne B. Freeman, ed., *Alexander Hamilton: Writings* (New York: Library of America, 2001) (hereafter Freeman, AHW), 3.

2. AH to James McHenry, February 18, 1781, in Freeman, AHW, 97.

3. Quoted on back cover of Jacob E. Cooke, ed., *The Reports of Alexander Hamilton* (New York: Harper & Row, 1964).

4. AH to Charles Cotesworth Pinckney, December 22, 1799, in Freeman, AHW, 922.

5. Quoted in Walter Stahr, *John Jay: Founding Father* (New York: Hambledon and London, 2005), 361.

6. AH to Charles Cotesworth Pinckney, December 29, 1802, in Freeman, AHW, 994–95.

Chapter 2

1. AH, "A Full Vindication of the Measures of the Congress" (December 15, 1774), in Freeman, AHW, 10–43 (at 12).

2. AH, "The Farmer Refuted . . ." (February 3, 1775), in Richard B. Morris, ed., *Alexander Hamilton and the Founding of the Nation* (New York: Harper Torchbooks/Harper & Row, 1969), 8–19 (quotation at 15).

3. AH, "A Second Letter from Phocion" (1784), in Morris, ed., *Hamilton*, quotation at 24.

4. Ibid.

5. AH to George Washington, September 15, 1790, in Morris, ed., *Hamilton*, 403.

6. AH, "Americanus No. 1" (February 1, 1794), in Morris, ed., *Hamilton*, 417–18.

7. TJ to JM, September 21, 1795, quoted in Merrill D. Peterson, *Thomas Jefferson and the New Nation* (New York: Oxford University Press, 1971), 547.

8. AH to Charles Cotesworth Pinckney, December 29, 1802, in Freeman, AHW, 994–95.

Chapter 3

1. AH, "Report of the Annapolis Convention" (September 14, 1786) in Freeman, AHW, 142–45 (quotation at 144).

2. AH, "Plan of Government" (June 18, 1787), in Freeman, AHW, 149–50; AH, "Speech in the Constitutional Convention on a Plan of Government" (June 18, 1787), in Freeman, AHW, 151–66.

3. AH, "Conjectures on the Constitution" (late September 1787), in Freeman, AHW, 167–70.

4. AH, *The Federalist* No. 69 (March 14, 1788) and *The Federalist* No. 70 (March 15, 1788), in Freeman, AHW, 366–73 and 374–82.

5. AH, *The Federalist* Nos. 78–83 (May 28, 1788), in Freeman, AHW, 420–66.

6. AH, *The Federalist* No. 85, in Freeman, AHW, 478–84 (quotation at 484).

7. AH, "Opinion on the Constitutionality of a National Bank" (February 22, 1791), in Freeman, AHW, 613–46.

8. AH, Letter to Gouverneur Morris, February 29, 1802, in Freeman, AHW, 985–86 (quotation at 986).

Chapter 4

1. AH to Angelina Schuyler Church [January 7, 1790], *Founders Online*, National Archives, https://founders.archives.gov/documents/Hamilton/01-06-02-0072. [Original source: *The Papers of Alexander Hamilton*, vol. 6, *December 1789–August 1790*, ed. Harold C. Syrett (New York: Columbia University Press, 1962), 50.]

2. AH, "Report on Public Credit" [January 9, 1790], in Freeman, AHW, 531–74.

3. AH, "Report on a National Bank" [December 13, 1790], in Freeman, AHW, 575–622,

4. AH, "Opinion on the Constitutionality of a National Bank" [February 22, 1791], in Freeman, AHW, 613–46.

5. AH, "Report on the Subject of Manufactures" [December 5, 1791], in Freeman, AHW, 647–734.

6. TJ, Letter to P. S. du Pont de Nemours [January 18, 1802], in Merrill D. Peterson, ed., *Thomas Jefferson: Writings* (New York: Library of America, 1984), 1099–1101 (quotation at 1101).

Chapter 5

1. AH to Elias Boudinot, July 11, 1778, in Freeman, AHW, 33–37 (quotation at 36).

2. AH, *The Federalist* No. 74, in Freeman, AHW, 400–2 (quotation at 400).

3. AH, *Pacificus* No. I (June 29, 1793), in Freeman, AHW, 803–9 (quotation at 809).

Chapter 6

1. The correspondence between Burr and Hamilton, and supporting documents, from June 18 through July 29, 1804, may be seen in Freeman, ed., AHW, 1008–91.

2. "Statement by Nathaniel Pendleton" (July 19, 1804), in Freeman, AHW, 1028–30 (quotation at 1029).

3. "Statement by William P. Van Ness" (July 21, 1804), in Freeman, AHW, 1030–31 (quotation at 1031).

Epilogue

1. AH, *The Federalist* No. 24 (December 19, 1787), in Freeman, AHW, 258–63 (quotation at 261).

FURTHER READING

The best way to get to know Alexander Hamilton is begin with his writings. The authoritative edition is Harold C. Syrett, Jacob E. Cooke, and Barbara Chernow, eds., *The Papers of Alexander Hamilton*, 27 vols. (New York: Columbia University Press, 1961–1987). See also Julius Goebel and Joseph H. Smith, eds., *The Law Practice of Alexander Hamilton*, 5 vols. (New York: Columbia University Press, 1964–1980). Hamilton's papers appear on three websites: Rotunda—https://www.upress.virginia.edu/rotunda (by subscription); Founders Online (National Archives)—http://founders.archives.gov (open access); and the Library of Congress—https://www.loc.gov/collections/alexander-hamilton-papers/ (open access).

Joanne B. Freeman, ed., *Alexander Hamilton: Writings* (New York: Library of America, 2001), is the best one-volume selection (and the source of most of this volume's endnotes); a useful abridged version is Joanne B. Freeman, ed., *The Essential Hamilton: Letters and Other Writings* (New York: Library of America, 2017). The best older compilation is Richard B. Morris, ed., *Alexander Hamilton and the Founding of the Nation* (New York: Harper & Row, 1957; rev. paperback ed., New York: Harper Torchbooks, 1969). See also Richard B. Vernier, ed., *The Revolutionary Writings of Alexander Hamilton* (Indianapolis: Liberty Fund, 2008); Alexander Hamilton, *Practical Proceedings in the Supreme Court of the State of New-York* (New York: American Lawyer Media, 2004) (text from Goebel and Smith, eds., *The Law Practice of Alexander Hamilton*, cited above); and E. P. Panagopoulos, ed., *Alexander Hamilton's Pay Book* (Detroit: Wayne State University Press, 1964). Hamilton's *Reports* as the nation's first secretary of the Treasury are available in Columbia's edition of his *Papers* and in the Library of America's editions of his *Writings,* and on Rotunda and Founders Online; there are also paperback editions of the *Reports,* notably that edited by Jacob E. Cooke (New York: Harper Torchbooks, 1964). The best editions of *The Federalist* are Jacob E. Cooke, ed., *The Federalist* (Middletown, CT: Wesleyan University Press, 1961); Clinton Rossiter, ed., *The Federalist Papers* (New York: Mentor Books/NAL, 1961) (new edition by Charles Kesler, 1987); and Benjamin F. Wright, ed., *The Federalist* (Cambridge, MA: Belknap Press of Harvard University Press/John Harvard Library, 1961).

The most popular biography is Ron Chernow's massive *Alexander Hamilton* (New York: Penguin Press, 2004). Older, valuable biographies include Forrest McDonald, *Alexander Hamilton* (New York: W. W. Norton, 1979); John Chester Miller, *Alexander Hamilton: Portrait in Paradox* (New York: Harper & Row, 1959); and Broadus Mitchell, *Alexander Hamilton,* 2 vols. (New York: Macmillan, 1957, 1962), the last being the most thorough scholarly biography, abridged as *Alexander Hamilton: A Concise Biography* (New York: Oxford University Press, 1976; repr., New York: Barnes & Noble Books, 1999). See also Michael E. Newton, *Alexander Hamilton: The Formative Years* (Phoenix, AZ: Eleftheria Publishing, 2015), and Michael E. Newton, *Discovering Hamilton: New Discoveries in the Lives of Alexander Hamilton, His Family, Friends, and Colleagues, from Various Archives around the World* (Phoenix, AZ: Eleftheria Publishing, 2019). See also John P. Kaminski, ed., *Alexander Hamilton: From Obscurity to Greatness* (Madison: Published for the Center for the Study of the American Constitution by Wisconsin Historical Society Press, 2018).

Important monographs include: Gerald Stourzh, *Alexander Hamilton and the Idea of Republican Government* (Stanford, CA: Stanford University Press, 1970); Clinton Rossiter, *Alexander Hamilton and the Constitution* (New York: Harcourt, Brace & World, 1964); Kate Elizabeth Brown, *Alexander Hamilton and the Development of American Law* (Lawrence: University Press of Kansas, 2017); Richard L. Green, *Alexander Hamilton's Public Administration* (Tuscaloosa: University of Alabama Press, 2019); Stephen F. Knott, *Alexander Hamilton and the Persistence of Myth* (Lawrence: University Press of Kansas, 2002); Harvey Flaumenhaft, *The Effective Republic: Administration and Constitution in the Thought of Alexander Hamilton* (Durham, NC: Duke University Press, 1992); Karl-Friedrich Walling, *Republican Empire: Alexander Hamilton on*

War and Free Government (Lawrence: University Press of Kansas, 1999); Lawrence S. Kaplan, *Alexander Hamilton: Ambivalent Anglophile* (Wilmington, DE: Scholarly Resources, 1999); John Lamberton Harper, *American Machiavelli: Alexander Hamilton and the Origins of U.S. Foreign Policy* (New York: Cambridge University Press, 2004); Lynton K. Caldwell, *The Administrative Theories of Hamilton & Jefferson: Their Contributions to Thought on Public Administration*, 2nd ed. (New York: Holmes & Meier, 1988); and Bower Aly, *The Rhetoric of Alexander Hamilton* (New York: Columbia University Press, 1941). See also James Willard Hurst, "Alexander Hamilton, Law-Maker," *Columbia Law Review* 78, no. 4 (April 1978): 483–547.

For studies of *The Federalist*, see David F. Epstein, *The Political Theory of The Federalist* (Chicago: University of Chicago Press, 1986); Albert Furtwangler, *The Authority of Publius: A Reading of The Federalist Papers* (Ithaca, NY: Cornell University Press, 1984); Richard B. Morris, *Witnesses at the Creation: Hamilton, Madison, Jay, and the Constitution* (New York: Holt, Rinehart & Winston, 1985); Gottfried Dietze, *The Federalist: A Classic on Federalism and Free Government* (Baltimore: Johns Hopkins University Press, 1962); Edwin Millican, *One United People; The Federalist Papers and the National Idea* (Lexington: University of Kentucky Press, 1990); Charles R. Kesler, ed., *Saving the Revolution: The Federalist Papers and the American Founding* (New York: Free Press/Macmillan, 1987); Garry Wills, *Explaining America: The Federalist* (New York: Doubleday, 1984); and Morton White, *Philosophy, The Federalist, and the Constitution* (New York: Oxford University Press, 1987). See also Trevor Colbourn, ed., *Fame and the Founding Fathers: Essays of Douglass Adair* (Indianapolis: Liberty Fund, 1999). The ultimate index for *The Federalist* is Thomas S. Engeman, Edward R. Erler, and Thomas B. Hofeller, eds., *The Federalist Concordance* (Chicago: University of Chicago Press, 1988).

For intellectual, historical, and political context, see Joanne B. Freeman, *Affairs of Honor: National Politics in the New Republic* (New Haven, CT: Yale University Press, 2001); Leonard D. White, *The Federalists: A Study in Administrative History 1789–1801* (New York: Macmillan, 1948); Lindsay M. Chervinsky, *The Cabinet: George Washington and the Creation of an American Institution* (Cambridge, MA: Belknap Press of Harvard University Press, 2020); Thomas K. McCraw, *The Founders and Finance: How Hamilton, Gallatin, and Other Immigrants Forged a New Economy* (Cambridge, MA: Belknap Press of Harvard University

Press, 2012); Robert E. Wright, *Hamilton Unbound: Finance and the Creation of the American Republic* (Westport, CT: Greenwood Press, 2002); Robert E. Wright, *One Nation under Debt: Hamilton, Jefferson, and the History of What We Owe* (New York: McGraw-Hill, 2008); Robert A. Ferguson, *Law and Letters in American Culture* (Cambridge, MA: Harvard University Press, 1984); Robert A. Ferguson, *Reading the Early Republic* (Cambridge, MA: Harvard University Press, 2004); Robert A. Ferguson, *The American Enlightenment* (Cambridge, MA: Harvard University Press, 1997); Richard B. Morris, *The Forging of the Union, 1781–1787* (New York: Harper & Row, 1987); Richard B. Morris, *Seven Who Shaped Our Destiny: The Founding Fathers as Revolutionaries* (New York: Harper & Row, 1973); and Henry Steele Commager, *Empire of Reason: How Europe Imagined and America Realized the Enlightenment* (Garden City, NY: Anchor Press/Doubleday, 1977).

For histories of Hamilton's time, see Alan Taylor, *American Revolutions: A Continental History, 1750–1804* (New York: W. W. Norton, 2016); Jonathan Israel, *The Expanding Blaze: How the American Revolution Ignited the World, 1775–1848* (Princeton, NJ: Princeton University Press, 2017); Gordon S. Wood, *Empire of Liberty: A History of the Early Republic. 1789–1815* (New York: Oxford University Press, 2009); Robert L. Middlekauff, *The Glorious Cause: The American Revolution, 1763–1789*, rev. ed. (New York: Oxford University Press, 2007); Stanley Elkins and Eric L. McKitrick, *The Age of Federalism 1788–1804* (New York: Oxford University Press, 1993); and John Chester Miller, *The Federalist Era, 1789–1800* (New York: Harper Brothers, 1960). See also R. B. Bernstein, *The Founding Fathers: A Very Short Introduction* (New York: Oxford University Press, 2015); Dennis C. Rasmussen, *Fears of a Setting Sun: The Disillusionment of America's Founders* (Princeton, NJ: Princeton University Press, 2021); and Akhil Reed Amar, *The Words That Made Us: America's Constitutional Conversation, 1780–1840* (New York: Basic Books, 2021).

INDEX

For the benefit of digital users, indexed terms that span two pages (e.g., 52–53) may, on occasion, appear on only one of those pages.